Manchester EveningNews WEEKEND **GO**

Family Walks Guide Volume 3

A guide to another 45 splendid
walks based on the popular
Manchester Evening News
Saturday column

By John & Anne Nuttall

Acknowledgements

Published by Diverse Media Ltd, 164 Deansgate, Manchester M60 2RD
Tel: 0161-211 2633; fax: 0161-839 1488; e-mail: citylife@mcr-evening-news.co.uk;
website: www.manchesteronline.co.uk

Managing Editor: Mike Hill
Designer: Robert Langley
Text & Photos: John & Anne Nuttall ©
Maps: Dick Graham
Front and back cover photographs: John Nuttall ©
website: www.nuttalls.com
With special thanks to Eric Jackson, Marcus Graham and the Diverse Media marketing team.

Published in April 2000.
Printed and Bound by MFP Design and Print, Manchester.

ISBN: 0 9537411 0 9

Contents

Foreword

*A*s dawn rose over the Peak District on 1 January 2000, two people crawled out of their tent, pitched the previous evening on the snowy dome of Bleaklow, and walked to the summit cairn. Beneath them, in the valleys, the cloud and mist rolled around obscuring the hangovers of ordinary mortals, and John and Anne Nuttall were bathed in the almost supernatural light.

To say John and Anne are keen walkers is like saying Jack Duckworth is keen on the gee-gees: they are not keen, they are passionate, with an almost religious fervour about their desire to spread the gospel of country walks.

But most important of all, they are not snobbish or elitist about walking. For them, a stroll around a lake and a country house followed by a tea shop cuppa is the equal to any strenuous scramble up a rocky mountain topped off with sarnies and a flask.

They stride around the North West seeking out new paths, measuring distances, photographing views, examining bus and train timetables, chatting to locals about the flora, fauna and local history, and they distil all this knowledge and expertise into their various columns, books, and CDs.

Occasionally they bump into people who are following one of their routes using a previous edition of this book, or who simply recognise them from their Saturday column in the Manchester Evening News.

Indeed, on that sunny New Year's Day, they met some walkers on Higher Shelf Stones, another local 2000 footer. The people were millennially resolved to conquer all the 'Nuttalls', ie. 2000 foot summits in England and Wales, and this was Number 1 on the list. "That's our list," said John, with just a hint of pride.

And it is with just a hint of pride that I sign off as Managing Editor of this mini-series. Editing this third volume of yet another 45 startlingly good walks has again whetted my appetite for the high hills and low valleys of the region, and I hope to bump into readers (and John and Anne) this summer.

Another editor will put the fourth volume to bed in September, and I will be first in line for a copy. In the meantime, keep on plodding on up hill and down dale.

Mike Hill
Managing Editor (emeritus)

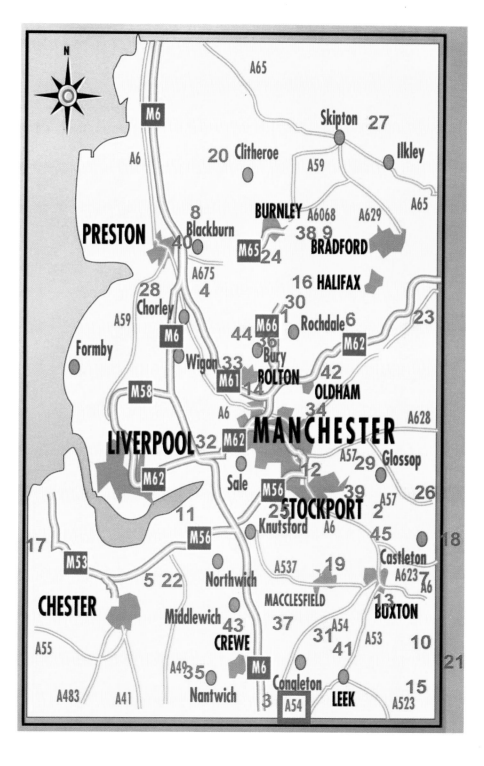

WAUGH AND PEACE

LOCATION: 5 miles north of Bury

START: Fisherman's Retreat, off A56. Follow signs from Shuttleworth along Bye Road. Please use Bottom Car Park

DISTANCE: 5½ miles

GRADE: Moderate

TIME: 3 hours

BUS: From Bury 90

MAP: Outdoor Leisure - South Pennines, Landranger 109

REFRESHMENTS: Fisherman's Retreat

Sheep on Scout Moor

Tucked down a winding lane, just off the busy M66 near Ramsbottom, the Fisherman's Retreat is a haven for walkers. Here anglers bend their rods over old mill lodges, while above this popular pub rise the grassy slopes of Scout Moor. Old coal roads and ancient tramways lead enticingly away from the valley, and soon you are up on the hills with extensive views and only the song of the lark for company. On a little alpine path, high above a deep ravine, the setting is poetic, and indeed this is the spot where Edwin Waugh came to write his verse, seated in 'a nook beside yon spring'.

THE ROUTE

From the Fisherman's Retreat, walk back down the track for about 100 yards, and turn right along the narrow Riding Head Lane. Gradually gaining height, the path leads uphill past Lodge Mill, then reaching the houses of Turn Village, you keep straight on up the grassy track. On meeting Rochdale Road, go right for a few yards to a small ladder over the wall, way-marked Rossendale Way, and cross the field to a stile.

Turning right to follow the old colliery road, you look down on Lime Leach, an 18th century loomshop still with its flight of 'takin'-in' steps, while looking back, Holcombe Moor is identified by the 1852 Peel Monument.

The Coal Road, which predates the later tramways, climbs steadily round the slopes of Scout Moor, and soon there is a grand view of the remote Upper Cheesden Valley. A waterfall tumbles in the clough amid traces of old coal pits and, as the moor opens out, the cross on the top of Whittle Pike comes into view. This was erected in memory of Flying Officer Geoffrey Molyneux, a local scout leader, killed in 1955.

Although the OS map still shows Great Lodge, which regulated the water for the mills, only a marsh remains, for the dam was removed 13 years ago. Continuing through a couple of gritstone gateposts, the Rossendale Way then begins to descend beside a ruined wall.

Crossing the stream, the airy path contours the steep slopes of a dramatic ravine, high above

Scout Moor High Level Reservoir, which was completed in 1909. Winter Hill can now be seen, while beyond the huge whale-back of Cowpe Low lie the Bowland Fells.

Waugh's Well is a convenient stopping point beside the path with a comfortable seat, and just round the corner are the ruins of Foe Edge Farm, where the dialect poet often stayed.

Just beyond is a concrete Water Board track, and you follow this downhill past the dam, forking right and down to cross Scout

Scout Moor High Level Resevoir

Moor Brook. A short ascent brings you to a dismantled tramway and this rather boggy track, still with the occasional rail and sleeper, is followed down the valley.

Keep on the lower tramway, which passes below the quarry spoil of Scout Moor Quarries, then reaching a wall, you follow it uphill and turn right. Crossing the new quarry road, keep straight on, with little sign of a path, to meet a sunken way below the stone wall and follow this down to New Gate Brook.

Stone slabs provide a bridge and, turning right, you cross a stile to the white house. A track then leads out to the main road where you turn left, past the Plane Tree Inn, then right down Lodge Mill Lane to rejoin the outward route.

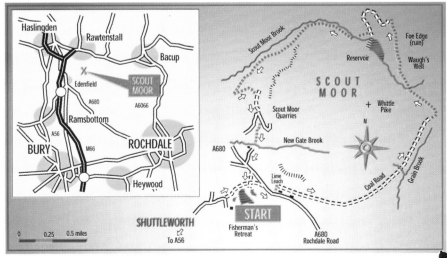

CRUEL TO BE KINDER

Tunstead Clough Farm

LOCATION: 4 miles east of New Mills

START: Bowden Bridge car park, 1 mile east of Hayfield on Kinder Road, toilets

DISTANCE: 6 miles

GRADE: Strenuous, with a steep ascent

TIME: Four hours

MAP: Outdoor Leisure - Dark Peak, Landranger 110

REFRESHMENTS: Pack a flask

Either you love Kinder or you hate it. There are no half measures about this high windswept plateau in the Dark Peak which dominates the skyline to the east of Manchester. The pièce de resistance is the Downfall, where the River Kinder throws itself over the cliff edge, and in a westerly gale the water is hurled back, forming a great plume in the air. Yet though Kinder can feel wild and remote, on a sunny day it is a delightful walk along the plateau rim, amid rocks carved into weird sculptures by the weather of 10,000 years.

THE ROUTE

From Bowden Bridge Quarry, with its bronze plaque commemorating the 400 ramblers who gathered here for the 1932 Kinder Mass Trespass, continue up the tarmac Kinder Road to the waterworks gates. Here you fork right, and then take the path beside the River Kinder, where white-throated dippers do aerobics on the stones. Re-crossing the river at a metal bridge, the footpath goes through a small gate by the entrance to the Treatment Works and climbs the cobbled way.

Soon Kinder Reservoir comes into view and ahead is the rocky amphitheatre of Kinder Downfall. Reaching William Clough, you go over the footbridge and follow the little trod which sets off steeply uphill. After crossing a stream, the path forks right, then it's a head down plod up the grassy rib until at last you reach the plateau.

Kinder Scout comes from the Saxon 'Kyndwr Scut', meaning water over the edge: turning right, it is easy walking along the plateau rim. The next rocky buttress is known as the Armchair, and on the very edge of the drop is a strange, white-painted symbol which marks a sacred spot of the Aetherius Society. The initials GK are those of their leader, George King.

The whole of Greater Manchester is now in view and on a clear day the distant South Pennines can be seen, while below is the Mermaid's Pool. Legend says that if you see a mermaid there on Easter Sunday, you will live forever!

You are now following the Pennine Way and, crossing a fence erected by the National Trust to control the sheep, the path continues to the deep indentation where the River Kinder tumbles over the rocks. This is a good spot for lunch, but keep an eye on the sheep which will have their noses in your rucksack if they get half a chance.

Top of the downfall

Crossing the infant river, continue round the edge for another half mile to the head of Red Brook. Here you leave the plateau to follow a little path downhill on the far side of the ravine. The path meanders across the slope above Cluther Rocks, where there was once a smithy and a millstone quarry. Keeping to the higher path, you contour the hillside before slanting down beneath Kinderlow End to a gate in the fence.

Continue beside the wall to the next gate, then keeping left, go through the gap and on down across the fields. It is an easy descent over a series of stiles to the 17th century Tunstead Clough Farm. Go round to the left of the buildings, then follow the farm track down to join a metalled road. Turning right beside the River Sett, this leads back to its confluence with the River Kinder at the ancient Bowden Bridge.

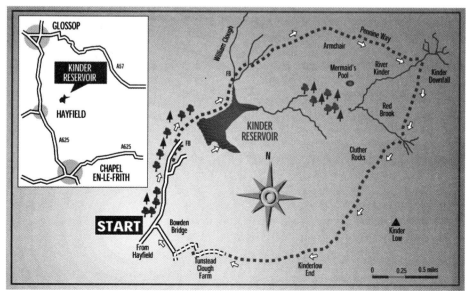

WALK 3: CHESHIRE RING & LAWTON WOODS (5 MILES, EASY)
BLOOD THICKER THAN WATER

The Tavern

LOCATION: 5 miles south of Congleton

START: Bleeding Wolf on the A34 at Scholar Green. Park behind pub

DISTANCE: 5 (or 3) miles

GRADE: Easy

TIME: 2½ hours

TRAIN: Kidsgrove

MAP: Pathfinder 792, Landranger 118

REFRESHMENTS: Bleeding Wolf

With its springtime sea of bluebells, Lawton Woods, on the fringe of the Potteries, is a delight. Set between the southern arms of the Cheshire Ring canals, which intertwine before disappearing into the dank depths of the Harecastle Tunnel, the secluded valley lies behind a Norman church in the grounds of the ruined Lawton Hall. The family came by their estate when King John, after being rescued from a wolf by a local peasant, granted him as much land as he could walk round, and the Bleeding Wolf was built on the spot where the wolf was slain.

THE ROUTE

From the Bleeding Wolf, cross the A34 and turn right to Moss Lane where a flight of steps leads down to the Macclesfield Canal. Opened in 1831, this was one of the last canals to be built. Turning right, the towpath leads under Bridge 95, with its pile of 'stop planks', used to block off the canal for draining. Then after the aqueduct over the A50, you come to the Canal Fly-over. Here the short walk turns down the steps to join the Trent & Mersey Canal.

The longer walk, however, continues along the Hall Green branch canal, crossing Bridge 96 by the Boat Painters yard. The two canals now run parallel to each other, and passing the moorings of Red Bull Basin, you soon arrive at Harding's Wood Junction where the waterways join.

Turning right over Bridge 98, it is now out and back to visit the Harecastle Tunnel. The tomato soup colour of the Trent & Mersey Canal is rust, not from the boats, but from iron oxide in the tunnel rock. Passing Kidsgrove Station, you arrive at the twin entrances. Although Brindley's 1775 tunnel has been closed, Telford's tunnel, constructed 70 years later, is working and a one-way system operates.

Returning to Harding's Wood Junction, cross over at the twin locks by The Tavern. These locks are an unusual feature of this canal, which has 24 pairs in the next seven miles. Continue along

12

the towpath past another set of locks and under the aqueduct then, reunited with the Short Route, you pass the Red Bull. One of the twin locks here was filled in when the road was widened, but just beyond the bridge is a whitewashed warehouse, built to store farm produce.

After passing two more pairs of locks, the canal bends right and goes under a concrete road bridge then, in 200 yards, you turn right over a stile to Lawton Church. Standing on a Saxon

Boat Painter

mound, this has an original Norman doorway and the tower dates from 1540.

Follow the churchyard wall left for about 70 yards, then cross the field to a stile into Lawton Woods. Bluebells are now a protected species, but here they flourish in profusion along with pink purslane and other woodland flowers.

Just before the footbridge you turn right beside the stream, then a way-mark points up the slope and the path goes along the top of the bank. Finally, tunnelling through rhododendrons, the path emerges above the Fish Pond and you turn left. Keep straight on, by a stand of tall beech trees, then crossing a track you can either follow the main path, or choose the prettier way which loops right, joining a maze of little paths through the bluebell wood.

Reaching the houses, make your way out to the main road, then the Bleeding Wolf pub is only a short distance away to the left.

TOWER OF POWER

Darwen Tower

LOCATION: 8 miles north of Bolton
START: Roddlesworth Information Centre car park, Tockholes, off A675, toilets
DISTANCE: 4 miles
GRADE: Moderate
TIME: 2 hours
NOTE: Information Centre open Sun & BH, also Wed & Sat pm
BUS: Direct from Bolton 535 (Sun only)
MAP: Explorer - West Pennine Moors, Landranger 103
REFRESHMENTS: Royal Arms

Like a giant spaceship poised ready for take-off, Darwen Tower stands proudly atop the moor. Officially, it was built to mark Queen Victoria's Diamond Jubilee, but for many it celebrated the freeing of Darwen Moor, a famous victory in 1896 over an oppressive landowner. Set high above Darwen, with a view of the Welsh mountains and the Lake District fells, the moor has the appeal of the wild Pennines, while the climb to the top of the tower is an experience not to be missed.

THE ROUTE

Crossing the stile in the far corner of the Information Centre car park, turn left to join the track to Ryal Fold. Just after the bend, you go through a little wooden gate and follow the fence down across the field towards the 1854 Earnsdale Reservoir, with its shelter belt of Scots pine.

From a stile in the field corner, a grassy track leads up to an ancient metal whirligig gate, then with a little more effort, a broad track is reached where you turn left. Now the view is extensive, with Blackburn ahead and in the distance lies Pendle Hill.

Reaching the 100-year-old Waterman's Cottage, fork right up the concrete waterworks track. Leaving this at the bend, a footpath contours across the hillside to join another track where you turn right and go through a metal gate onto the open moor.

The track veers away right, but keeping straight on uphill it's a steady climb, and soon Darwen, with its huge India Mill chimney, can be seen far below. Then a carved stone sign points right and the path makes a bee-line for the 86ft octagonal tower.

The Jubilee Tower, which was renovated in 1972, is magnificent, and climbing to the top is both an adventure and an education, for all the surrounding hills can be identified from neat diagrams on the topmost parapet.

14

Next you follow the good path which sets off across the moor from behind the tower. After crossing an area which was devastated by fire in 1996, turn left at the T-junction to the edge of the moor. The heather covered spoil heaps are those of an old drift mine, from which a mile-long tramway carried coal down into Darwen.

Don't follow the edge, but turn sharply back to the right along a path which crosses the top of the grassy moor. In about half a mile, a gate is reached, then beyond you fork right down to a clump of trees known as the Lyons Den. Only a few grassy mounds remain to show where John Lyon, the local strongman, once lived.

The track follows Stepback Clough, so named when Oliver Cromwell ordered his troops to retreat from here in bad weather. It can certainly be 'Two top-coats colder', as the man said whom we met up here, but in the warmth of the April sunshine, the coltsfoot was in flower, while the Peacock Butterflies thought summer had arrived.

Tower signpost

Continuing down the wooded valley, you pass a capped mine shaft and just below there was once a row of cottages. Then crossing the stile by a gate, keep straight on along the good track until, emerging from the trees, you fork right to the cottages and the Royal Arms.

Earnsdale Reservoir

Waterman's Cottage

Ryal Fold

PH

START

Sunnyhurst Hey Reservoir

Darwen Tower

To A675

Darwen Moor

BLACKBURN

DARWEN

Ryal Fold

A666

A675

X

DARWEN MOOR

Stepback Clough

N

Scale
0   0.25   0.5 miles

IT'S A CLIFF-HANGER

Jacob's Ladder

LOCATION: 3 miles south of Runcorn

START: Beacon Hill car park. Take the B5152 from Frodsham, turn right along Manley Road, & right again at Simons Lane

DISTANCE: 4½ (or 3) miles

GRADE: Easy, but with a short, rocky descent

TIME: 2½ hours

MAP: Pathfinder 757, Landranger 117

REFRESHMENTS: Pack a flask

Cheshire is not famed for its mountains, but standing on the edge of the precipitous sandstone outcrops at Mersey View, high above Frodsham, you feel on top of all things. With densely wooded slopes, hollowed-out caves, an Iron Age hill fort and extensive views across the estuary, there is much to explore. And though the first part of the walk, along quiet green lanes, is tame enough, the ascent of Jacob's Ladder turns it into an adventure. Here a staircase, hewn out of the rock, climbs the eroded cliff face - but don't worry, there's an easy way round for the non-mountaineers!

THE ROUTE

Turn left out of the car park and walk back along Simons Lane, then just after Frodsham Golf Club, take the footpath on the right by the Practice Area. Following the Delamere Way (a 20-mile long-distance trail), the path goes along the field edge and by a high fence, while to the right are the distant mudflats of the Mersey. Reaching a farm track, continue across the field to Manley Road, where you turn right on the grassy verge.

At Shepherds Houses, the Short Route turns right, to join the Sandstone Trail in the woods. The Main Route, however, goes left, up the sandy track to Harrol Edge with its grass-banked reservoir. Then, meeting the tarmac road, you turn right to follow a track edged with cherry and hawthorn, wild roses, brambles and frothy white cow parsley.

Joining a quiet lane, you turn right then, at the next junction, you fork right to descend past the barn conversions at Riley Bank. Crossing the road to a ladder stile, follow the footpath down beside the fence into a pretty little valley, where red campion blooms beneath bracken-covered slopes. Continue down the valley until, after crossing a stile, the path kinks right, and round the field edge, to meet the Sandstone Trail.

Turning right, the track leads gently uphill by the wooded slopes of Snidley Moor. The pigs in the adjacent field, rooting happily in the sandy soil, barely glanced up as we followed the old sunken lane up through the rhododendrons.

At a T-junction, the Short Route is rejoined and you turn left along the field edge. Woodhouse Hill Fort, with its low earth ramparts, lies hidden in the trees, then the Trail bends left and over the brow of the escarpment to a seat. From the top of the 300 million-year-old Triassic sandstone cliffs you look across to Helsby Hill, Stanlow Refinery and the Helsby and Frodsham marshes.

The Trail now goes just below the rim of the escarpment, then follows the cliff top before descending the rocky staircase of Abraham's Leap. Continuing beneath the red sandstone outcrops, you come to Jacob's Ladder. This adventurous scramble is easier than it looks, but a stepped path to the right avoids all difficulties.

The memorial at Mersey View

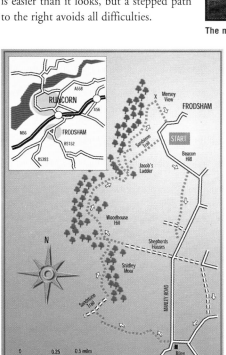

Reaching a signpost, don't go back to the car park, but instead continue along the top of the wood. Passing a viewpoint - beware of the quarry ahead - the view opens out again across the Mersey Estuary. A little further and you come to Mersey View and the War Memorial where a topograph points out the curve of the Widnes-Runcorn Bridge, the distant Winter Hill and the Welsh mountains. Finally, the higher path leads out to ornate wrought iron gates, where you turn right up the road to the car park.

IT'S NOT THAT DESPERATE, DAN

LOCATION: Midway between Rochdale and Halifax

START: On the moors at the A58/B6138 road junction

DISTANCE: 8 (or 3) miles

GRADE: Easy

TIME: 4 hours

BUS: From Rochdale: 528

MAP: Outdoor Leisure - South Pennines, Landranger 103 & 109

REFRESHMENTS: White House

Warland Resevoir

'The most desolate, wild, and abandoned country in all England,' wrote Daniel Defoe of Blackstone Edge early in the 18th century. But fashions change and now these high moors above Rochdale are a favourite with ramblers. Meadow pipits, wheatears and larks call above a miniature lakeland of reservoirs which once supplied the Rochdale Canal, while meandering drains contour the hillside, making very easy walking. An eight mile tramp, over remote moorland on good paths, and with no ascent at all - this walk must be unique.

THE ROUTE

From the A58, walk down the B-road towards Mytholmroyd beside Blackstone Edge Reservoir. Then, entering West Yorkshire (have your passports ready!), you turn left 300 yards beyond, along the waterworks track.

The walk follows the concrete-lined Byron Edge Drain, with extensive views over the moor to the north until, passing three black sluice gates, you reach White Holme Reservoir dam. Here the Short Route goes left to skirt the reservoir, but the Main Route turns right on the Reservoir Circuit along the curving dam.

The long, whale-backed Great Manshead Hill, on the far side of the B-road, looks very impressive, and it's worth noting there is now a permissive path running the whole length of the ridge.

Crossing the footbridge over the spillway, the path continues along the dam and beside a narrow arm of the reservoir, but apart from a low, rocky outcrop only an ocean of tussock grass, crowberry and heather stretches ahead. More sluice gates are passed and the sandy path, much softer underfoot, continues past a fine cairn, along White Holme Drain onto Turkey Holes and Higher House Moor.

Below are the twin-pointed cairns of Two Lads, then, as the path bends left, Stoodley Pike comes into view. The original monument, erected in 1814, fell down and this is the third tower to be built on the hilltop.

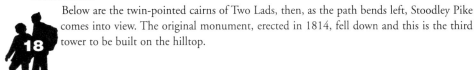

18

Still following the narrowing drain, you come to the Cloven Stone and just beyond is a ruined shooting box with a great, stone table. The drain now runs in a half-buried concrete pipe as the path continues above Withens Clough Reservoir. On the slopes of Bird Nest Hill, the drain emerges again and on the skyline to the left are the prominent Holder Stones.

Ahead in the distance, the windmills on the Long Causeway signal with their white arms, and reaching the Pennine Way, you turn left. A fine set of double lock-gates enlivens the waterway, and here the track bends left.

Although the track continues beside Warland Reservoir, it is more attractive along the eastern shore, and crossing the drain you follow a narrow footpath through the heather below Stony Edge. A little clapper bridge spans a now dry watercourse and the path continues over the tussocky grass, while in the distance is the trig point on Little Holder Stones.

County boundary

After following the embankment above Light Hazzles Reservoir, the path crosses a little footbridge to rejoin the Pennine Way, where you turn left. Reaching the end of the reservoir, the Short Route joins the track and you continue past a disused quarry, which supplied stone for the dams, while to the south is the blue expanse of Hollingworth Lake.

At last, the 17th century White House inn, which was purpose built for travellers, appears ahead: then, after passing beneath the dam of Blackstone Edge Reservoir, you reach the main road and turn left, back to the start of the walk.

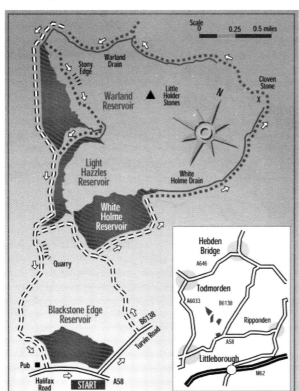

19

BRIDGE OVER THE RIVER WYE

River Wye

LOCATION: 6 miles east of Buxton

START: Miller's Dale Station car park, off B6049, toilets

DISTANCE: 4 miles

GRADE: Moderate, but Monk's Dale is rough underfoot and slow-going

TIME: 2½ hours

MAP: Outdoor Leisure - White Peak, Landranger 119

REFRESHMENTS: Angler's Rest, Wriggly Tin & Wormhill

Monk's Dale must be one of the slowest miles in all of the White Peak. But it's not just the rocky path that delays progress, for this valley is a botanist's paradise. Cowslips and early purple orchids cover the banks, violets bloom beneath the hawthorn bushes, while later in the year there are rock roses and sweet-smelling thyme. Yet the walk is not all tough-going, for first you stroll beside the swift-flowing River Wye before climbing to the pretty village of Wormhill, birthplace of James Brindley, the Father of the English canal system. You even pass two tea rooms and a pub - what more could you want!

THE ROUTE

Go round to the back of the station and turn right along the disused railway. The line, which once linked London and Manchester, was built in the days of intense inter-company rivalry and, like an alpine railway, has many tunnels and great viaducts across the river.

Reaching the end of the old platform, you turn left down a stepped path into Miller's Dale, then go right along the River Wye. Sandwiched between the steep slope of the railway embankment and the river, the path leads through the trees and under a high viaduct. Continue upstream to a blue-railed footbridge, but don't cross over.

Instead, turn right on a little path which slants up the hillside following a natural rocky shelf where many lime-loving flowers bloom. The path then veers right and climbs on until you emerge onto the road opposite Wormhill Hall, which has just celebrated its 300th birthday.

Turning left you come to a farmhouse selling refreshments, and here the route goes right, down the lane to the church, but first there is the Brindley Memorial. It's on the green, just beyond the junction, together with the village stocks, and commemorates the famous engineer, who was born in the adjacent hamlet of Tunstead in 1716.

Go down the lane past the 13th century church. This was restored in Victorian times, but don't miss the Saxon cross, topped by a sundial, in the churchyard. Turning left at the bend, a footpath follows the wall on the far side of the field up to a stile under a large hawthorn tree. Heading then diagonally left, you come to a narrow walled lane, set in a network of gleaming white walls which date from the Enclosure Acts. Meeting another ancient green lane you turn right through a small wooden gate and follow the old route down into Monk's Dale.

Reaching the valley bottom, turn right to enter the densely wooded Nature Reserve. The next half mile is very slow-going as the path meanders through the trees. Finally, just when you have decided it can't possibly be any further, a stile appears and you climb out into the open pasture.

The short-cropped turf comes as a pleasant contrast, with white drifts of meadow saxifrage. Keep to the higher path which, after dipping to meet the stream, climbs again past a little rocky outcrop where the spring cinquefoil can be found.

Crossing the footbridge, the path leads on down

Railway viaduct over the River Wye

the dale, then climbing out of the valley, you turn right. Follow the wall up to meet the road by the whitewashed Glebe Farm, then it's left down the road, back to Miller's Dale, the Wriggly Tin cafe and The Angler's Rest.

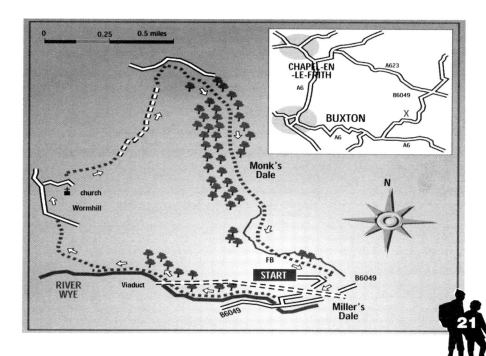

21

ROAMIN' AS ROMANS

LOCATION: 5 miles north of Blackburn

START: Off B6245. Turn right immediately before Ribchester Bridge and follow lane to Marles Wood Car Park (Grid Ref 675357)

DISTANCE: 4½ miles

GRADE: Easy

TIME: 2 hours

MAP: Explorer-West Pennine Moors, Landranger 103

REFRESHMENTS: Copster Green

Cottages at Copster Green

Swallows skimmed low over the fields as we climbed away from the old Roman road that led to Ribchester. Overhead, thunder clouds were building, but only a few drops fell as we reached the village of Copster Green. The name means settlement on a pointed hill, and there are extensive views over the Ribble Valley, while eastwards Pendle Hill dominates a landscape of green fields and quiet country lanes. But the best is saved till last, for after a gentle descent you walk beside the River Ribble through meadows full of yellow iris and woods carpeted with garlic-scented ramsons.

THE ROUTE

From the car park, go back onto the lane and turn right, then at the bend, take the footpath on the left. Keeping beside the wood, it is an easy climb, while looking back you can see the steep roof of Salesbury Hall, whose owners were Royalist supporters during the Civil War.

After about 400 yards, where the fence bends left, head diagonally right to a stile by a signpost at the top of the field. Now Ribchester is in view, a settlement which grew up on the site of the Roman fort. This is the only village built on the banks of the River Ribble.

Continuing across the next field, aim for the signpost which stands beside a pond planted with water-lilies. The right of way then goes parallel to the field boundary, but a good track follows the field edge, until you turn left down an old hawthorn-lined green lane.

Keep straight on through the farmyard and across the bridge, where the delicate pink purslane grows by the brook. The track bends right at Park Gate and passes a row of whitewashed terraced cottages. A short detour here, down the track to the right, brings you to Bolton Hall, a magnificent mansion built in 1655.

Reaching the main road in Copster Green, once a goose green ringed by handloom weavers' cottages, you turn left. Then after 200 yards go left again, up the tarmac drive past Copster Hall, dated 1615 and the oldest house in the village.

Follow the track on across the fields, with Pendle Hill looming in the eastern view, then reaching a gateway, way-marks point the way to a single plank footbridge. A short section of wall supports the stile ahead, then a ruined wall and the field boundary act as a guide to a wooden stile at the far end of the field.

The barns of Dinckley Grange are the next aiming point,

Bolton Hall

but just before you reach the farm, take the leftmost of the two stiles. A path leads out to the road opposite a red-brick house, where you turn right, then left by the former pub. Keep straight on at the junction to follow the quiet lane.

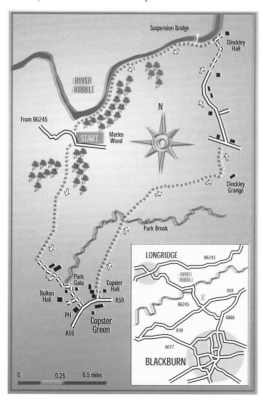

Passing the white gate, continue down the lane to the entrance of the 16th century Dinckley Hall, another Royalist stronghold, then turn left beside the River Ribble. Reaching the grand, white suspension bridge, which replaced a ferry, don't cross over but continue beside the river. These meadows are Open Access, so you can wander wherever you like.

A kissing gate leads into Marles Wood and the path follows the river to Sales Wheel, where the channel narrows. Then you turn left up the stepped concessionary footpath, back to the car park.

TAKE THE LIME LINE

Top of the aqueduct shaft

LOCATION: 3 miles north of Hebden Bridge

START: Layby on A6033, 1½ miles beyond Pecket Well

DISTANCE: 5 miles

GRADE: Moderate

TIME: 2½ hours

BUS: From Todmorden: 500

MAP: Outdoor Leisure - South Pennines, Landranger 103 & 104

REFRESHMENTS: Pack a flask

The experts from Bradford University must be expecting wet weather, for on the moors above Hebden Bridge is a laboratory built to measure the size of raindrops. The waterboard, too, are anticipating a downpour, for many reservoirs lie in the hollows. But it isn't always raining, and as we climbed the slopes of High Brown Knoll a heat-haze filled the valleys, while the sun shone out of an almost cloudless blue sky. Skylarks hovered overhead, curlews sang their warbling notes, and lapwings gave a display of aerobatics. On a fine sunny day, take a stroll around the high Calderdale moors, what could be nicer!

THE ROUTE

A few yards downhill from the lay-by, a bridleway, signed Limers Gate, sets off across the grassy moor. This was the route taken by pack-horses carrying lime from Yorkshire into Lancashire. After a short climb, you are on the top of Naze Hill. The view is extensive, with Stoodley Pike to the south, while to the north are the roofs of the university laboratory.

Continuing across the wild hilltop, a narrow, cairned path leads on towards the distant circling arms of the windmills on Ovenden Moor. A few rocks break the expanse of grass, while on the summit of High Brown Knoll is a fine rocking stone, a whitewashed trig point and a prominent standing stone.

Limers Gate bypasses the summit, and the route goes to the right of the trig point, then following way-marks you plod over the tussocky moor. Joining an obvious track, turn right and this leads to the stone-lined Catchwater Drain, which feeds Warley Moor Reservoir.

A little stone bridge spans the drain, and here you turn right to continue across the moor, whose Nardus grassland is now brightened by patches of bilberry and heather. The towers on the moor are airshafts for an underground aqueduct.

Crossing the stream in Back Clough, follow the ruined wall above Luddenden Dean, a

John on the Trig point, High Brown Knoll

secluded valley and the site of a medieval settlement. The route briefly becomes a sunken lane then, at a path junction by a line of shooting butts, you turn sharply back right to follow a sandy trod up onto the heather moor.

In a few yards, take the right fork and, keeping straight on, soon the Calder Valley comes into view. A stone trough marks Brigg Well Head Spring, then meeting the wall, you follow it past a cottage, with mullioned windows, where cloth was once woven.

Continuing under the slopes of Bog Eggs Edge, the path joins the Calderdale Way and leads on round the hillside, where kestrels hover in the up currents. Down below lies Pecket Well with its tall fustian mill chimney and miniature Stoodley Pike war memorial.

The Calderdale Way turns away downhill, but the route continues beside the wall until, passing Old Town Slack Farm and another aqueduct airshaft, you reach an old quarry. Go through the farm gate on the left, then turn right through a second gate and down the sandy track. At the junction, go right on the rough track, then at the bend, a gate on the right leads back onto the moor.

The grassy track stays beside the wall before cutting across the corner to follow the wall to Spinks Hill Farm. The farm track then leads across the fields back to the start of the walk.

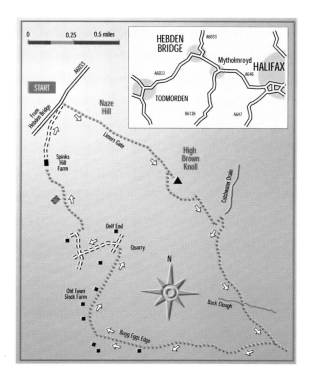

AWESOME WELLS

By Long Rake

LOCATION: 10 miles south east of Buxton

START: Follow signs to Youlgreave from A515, then to Picnic Area at Moor Lane (Grid ref 194645)

DISTANCE: 6 miles

GRADE: Moderate

TIME: 3 hours

MAP: Outdoor Leisure-White Peak, Landranger 119

REFRESHMENTS: Youlgreave

Below us, in the deep, green pools of Lathkill Dale, fat trout lay still, while by the shady banks moorhens and coots reared their downy young. Then joining the River Bradford, we followed it upstream past sparkling weirs where a flash of brilliant yellow revealed a grey wagtail. These dales are lovely throughout the summer, but the third week in June there is an extra delight, for the ancient lead mining settlement of Youlgreave celebrates its well dressing. With its springs, wells, and even a water tank decorated with flower petals, the village will be at its best.

THE ROUTE

From the car park entrance, turn right and walk down the road for a quarter of a mile, then take the footpath on the left. This crosses the field and then a strip of woodland, which conceals the chasm of Long Rake, an old lead mine.

Reaching the road - watch out for cars - the footpath continues across the fields, slanting right towards Over Haddon. Though the village looks very close, it is actually on the far side of the hidden Lathkill Dale. A muddy track then leads down to Meadow Place Grange. With its buildings set round a courtyard, this retains the plan of the monastic grange, which belonged to Leicester Abbey from the 12th century until the dissolution of the monasteries.

Go straight across the farmyard and over the next field to join a track which hairpins down into Lathkill Dale. Crossing the clapper bridge, turn right in front of the gleaming, white, water bailiff's lodge. The river, often dry in its upper reaches, emerges here at an extensive tufa deposit, a natural calcium carbonate only found in very pure limestone streams.

Climbing a little flight of steps, you look down on the green depths of the river. Then continuing through a meadow, popular with picnickers, you join the old turnpike road and turn right to cross the medieval Conksbury Bridge. The parapets are festooned in the purple flowers of ivy-leaved toadflax, which came originally from the Mediterranean.

Youlgreave Well Dressing

Follow the road for a few yards, then turn left on a path across the fields. Reaching the junction by Raper Lodge, keep straight on along the valley, but look back to see Coalpit Bridge, over which pack-horses carried coal from Chesterfield.

Next you arrive at the hamlet of Alport, where the Old Portway, an ancient trackway, forded the river. Here the Lathkill joins the River Bradford and, crossing straight over the road, by the 1793 bridge, you follow the River Bradford upstream. Passing Rheinstor, a climbing cliff which to mere mortals appears entirely without holds, you join a track and, continuing over the next road, stay beside the river.

Youlgreave is only a short detour, and a slanting path climbs the hill to the village which has an 800-year-old church, a couple of pubs and a Youth Hostel in the old Co-Op. The return to the river is down Holywell Lane past an excellent tea room.

Crossing the flat stone slab bridge, continue upstream through the sylvan dale, past a series of man-made fishponds. At the next bridge, you cross over and take the zigzag path up the hill. Joining the road, turn right, past the grand Lomberdale Hall, then, at the bend, a footpath leads up to join the higher road. Turn left, then in 100 yards, a path leads up the flower-decked hillside back to the picnic area.

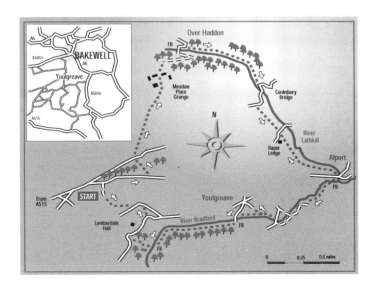

WALTON MOUNTAIN (NOT!)

LOCATION: 2 miles south of Warrington

START: Walton Hall Gardens car park. Turn off A56 at Walton Arms pub and go down Walton Lea Road, toilets

DISTANCE: 5 miles

GRADE: Easy

TIME: 2 ½ hours (allow longer if you visit the gardens)

BUS: From Warrington X30, 62 & 31

MAP: Pathfinder 739 & 740, Landranger 108 & 109

REFRESHMENTS: Moore & Heritage Centre café

Canoeists on the Bridgewater Canal

With foxgloves beside the canal and dog roses in the hedges, we felt in the depths of the countryside as we explored the quiet lanes and field paths on the fringe of Warrington. Swallows skimmed low over the Bridgewater Canal, lapwings flocked in the hay meadow, and in the distance a cuckoo called. Even the lovely formal gardens of Walton Hall were deserted. Where had everyone gone? The answer was the playground. Children swung high in the air and hurtled down the slide. Families lazed on the grass while brilliant blue peacocks strutted and called, and a friendly donkey dozed in the sun.

THE ROUTE

From the entrance to Walton Hall Gardens, go down the wooden steps to the Bridgewater Canal and turn right. Now rhododendrons overhang the quiet canal in its deep sandstone cutting, but once this was busy with horse-drawn boats on day trips from Manchester. Following the towpath through Higher Walton village, which dates back to the 12th century, you pass estate cottages built by Greenalls, once the local brewers. Then, after the moorings at Walton Bridge, the towpath continues under the new concrete Chester Road Bridge and wanders peacefully on, under Thomason's Bridge and past a picnic area by a spinney.

Passing Acton Grange Bridge, where towropes have cut into the wood protecting the bricks, the steaming cooling towers of Cuerdley Power Station appear on the skyline. At last you reach the village of Moore with its attractive Canal Side Cottages. Go under Moore Bridge, then leaving the canal, turn right back along the road, and cross the bridge. Taking the right fork, follow Hobb Lane, where pick marks show that it was hewn from solid rock, and Norton Water Tower comes into view.

Crossing the busy Chester Road (take care!), the footpath almost opposite leads over the field to Outer Wood, while the local landmark of Daresbury Laboratory Tower stands like the conning tower of a giant submarine.

Turn left at a signpost by the wood and continue across the field, then follow the edge of Row's Wood. Once part of the Walton Estate, this was densely planted with rhododendrons and bamboo to provide cover for game birds.

Reaching a kissing gate, the footpath cuts through the trees, then continues across the field to another kissing gate. Keeping left to the far corner, you join Warrington Road. Turn left on the grassy verge, then in 200 yards take the footpath on the right, signed Appleton Reservoir.

The path follows an expertly laid hedge, beside a hay meadow full of ox-eye daisies. At the far side, turn left and continue beside the wood to the field corner where a stile leads into a new plantation of assorted broad-leaved trees. Arriving at Appleton Reservoir, follow the embankment left. Built to serve industry,

Peacock in the childrens zoo

the reservoir is now disused and fishermen stand thigh-deep in water stocked with trout.

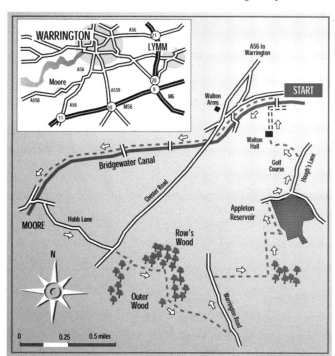

Emerging onto Park Lane turn right, then left down Hough's Lane. Watch for the Golfers Crossing Point where you go left to follow the edge of the golf course beside the wood to Walton Hall. It is then only a short stroll back to the start past the remains of the hall, which was built in the 1830s. The formal gardens are superb, but don't forget to visit the Children's Zoo and the Heritage

ESCAPE TO THE SECRET GARDEN

Didsbury Church

LOCATION: Didsbury, South Manchester.

START: Simon's Bridge car park at the end of Ford Lane. Turn off A5145 down Dene Road, then go immediately left

DISTANCE: 2½ miles

GRADE: Easy

TIME: 1½ hours

BUS: 42,40,157

TRAIN: East Didsbury

MAP: Landranger 109, Manchester A-Z

REFRESHMENTS: Cafe in park & The Didsbury pub

You don't expect to find cows in Didsbury, let alone a secret garden, but hidden behind the parish church is one of the gems of Manchester. Here paths and ancient pack-horse routes lead through woodland and across grassy meadows to the River Mersey. The slow flowing river, whose name means boundary in Anglo-Saxon, is home to herons and mallards, while wild flowers grow along the banks. But the highlight of the walk is the Botanical Gardens where stately trees look down on a mass of brilliant blooms in one of the finest rock gardens in the country.

THE ROUTE

From the far end of the car park, follow the surfaced footpath out to the river bank by Simon's Bridge. Built in 1901 by Henry Simon, the iron bridge replaced Northenden Ford on the line of an old saltway.

Turning left, you follow the lower path upstream beside the River Mersey whose steep artificial banks are to control flooding. Passing a memorial seat with a view across the river to Didsbury golf course, the broad track continues by the tree-lined Mersey. Tall pink-flowered Himalayan Balsam fringes the river, while blackberries bloom beside the purple nodding bells of comfrey, which was once used to help broken bones to heal.

Reaching the overhead pylons, and with the motorway in sight beyond, you turn left up a sandy track, then go immediately right beside the hawthorn hedge. A strip of woodland now separates you from the river, and most of the trees have been planted since 1973.

The pleasant track leads on to a crossroads where you turn left, past the flood storage notice, to continue beside the playing field. Edged by pink dog roses, the path follows a high embankment by Millgate Fields. For around 20 years, this land was used for refuse tipping, but now the land has been reclaimed. The path bends right, past Millgate Farm, which dates back to the 19th century, then you continue beside the flood storage basin, constructed in the 1970s.

Keep straight on at the next junction beside open grassland full of buttercups and clover, and continue straight on to a four-way junction where you take the rightmost stepped path into Stenner Woods.

Follow the board walk, which leads through the willow-shrouded wetland, until you emerge from the wood by Millgate Lane. Gate is the old word for road and there was a corn mill here as long ago as 1280.

Staying in the park, turn left along the good path past the Wild Flower Area into the Botanical Gardens. This land was donated to the public by Fletcher Moss, who lived in the old parsonage opposite Didsbury Church.

Fletcher Moss Garden

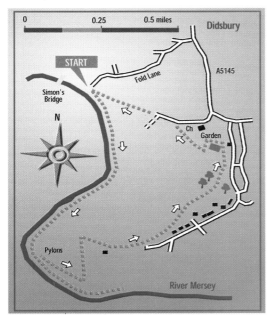

The route now goes to the right of the tennis courts and through the rock garden. There is a marvellous display, with every plant labelled, and the added distraction of a cafe. Emerging back into the park, go past the tennis courts and turn right on the tarmac path, out to Stenner Lane, by Didsbury Church, whose tower is dated 1620. There is a convenient pub next door.

Turn left along the road and keep straight on beyond the gate, past playing fields which in medieval times were cultivated in long, thin strips. Then the shady lane, an ancient trackway, leads back to the car park.

FOLLY GOOD SHOW

Bird's-foot-trefoil

LOCATION: Peak District

START: Buxton. Poole's Cavern car park, signed from A53, toilets

DISTANCE: 2½ miles

GRADE: Moderate

TIME: 1½ hours

NOTE: Poole's Cavern & Visitor Centre open daily (except in winter)

BUS: Trent Transpeak

TRAIN: Buxton station 1 mile

MAP: Outdoor Leisure - White Peak, Landranger 119

REFRESHMENTS: Buxton

Perched on the top of Grin Low, high above Buxton, stands the gleaming white limestone tower of Solomon's Temple. It is an irresistible attraction and the walk up through the woods to the flower-covered summit is delightful. Then, after climbing the steps that spiral up within the folly, you can visit Poole's Cavern, the only entirely natural show cave in Derbyshire. This is a walk in miniature. Dogs, children, grandparents, all will love it - and as a little extra, there's the added excitement of getting lost in Grin Wood!

THE ROUTE

From Poole's Cavern car park, climb the steps which lead up into Grin Low Woods, but on meeting the track ignore the sign pointing to Solomon's Temple and turn right, along the hillside. In a few yards, a path forks left, and you follow it through the beech trees along the edge of the wood, with extensive views over Buxton to the escarpment of Coombs Moss. This 100 acre wood was planted in 1820 by the 6th Duke of Devonshire to hide the scars of lime burning.

When the path starts to go downhill, fork left and continue on the level, ignoring paths to the left, to regain the edge of the wood. Then, reaching a wall corner, you turn left to climb through the trees to the fence which bounds Grin Quarry. (There is a maze of little paths and it is easy to go wrong, but if you get lost, just head uphill.)

Walking beneath the trees, loud with the insistent calls of chaffinches, you may hear the wood warbler or the drumming of the great-spotted woodpecker, and all seems entirely natural. Yet the hummocks are 400-year-old ash tips. By the end of the 18th century, the whole area was covered in a million tons of waste and the lime burners even made their homes in caves hollowed in the solidified spoil heaps.

Reaching the fence at the top of the wood, you turn left. Keep to the higher path as it meanders through the trees until steps lead up into a clearing where common spotted-orchids bloom. Then staying beside the fence, there is a surprise view of the huge quarry. Limestone was extracted here until 1972, but now kestrels nest on the cliffs and the quarry hides a caravan park.

Continue by the fence until a gate leads onto the open hillside, then follow the path by the wall. Solomon's Temple is now in view amid an alpine pasture bright with golden bird's-foot-trefoil. An ascent of the tower is a must, and a staircase leads to the turreted roof, where you look out on the Peak District hills. The folly was built in 1896 by Solomon Mycock, to provide work for

Solomon's Temple

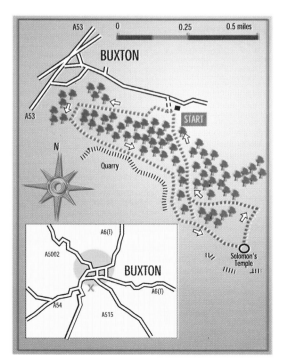

unemployed quarrymen. This was the site of a Neolithic tumulus, and excavations revealed six bodies and other remains, which are displayed in the Visitor Centre.

Heading now downhill towards Buxton, a squeezer stile in the wall leads into a flower-filled meadow, where you can hunt for the yellow mountain pansy. The hollowed mound is the 'frying pan', an old lime kiln with a 'handle' for the pack-horses which brought stone for burning.

An obvious five-barred gate on the left leads into the wood and you follow an old pack-horse track through the trees. Then, joining the main path, you turn downhill back to the steps, the Visitor Centre and Poole's Cavern.

HAVE WE GOT NEWTS FOR YOU

Ringley packhorse bridge and clock tower

LOCATION: Bolton

START: Moses Gate Country Park, off A6053, signed from Farnworth, toilets

DISTANCE: 6 ½ (or 2) miles

GRADE: Easy

TIME: 3 hours

BUS: 8, 9 & 28

TRAIN: Moses Gate Station, ½ mile

MAP: Pathfinder 712, Landranger 109

REFRESHMENTS: Ringley

Weaving its way through the trees, the Manchester, Bolton and Bury Canal plays a game of hide-and-seek above the wide meanders of the River Irwell. Lost to navigation over half a century ago, when its waters poured out in a catastrophic collapse, the canal is now a tranquil backwater among a network of ancient transport routes. With two pack-horse bridges, an old steam crane and a splendid aqueduct, this is an Industrial Archaeologist's dream, while the dereliction of the last century has mellowed into a magnificent site for orchid hunters.

THE ROUTE

From the iron gates of Rock Hall, go left beside the River Croal and follow the tarmac track to cross the red footbridge. Keeping right, steps lead up into the wood and you turn right on a broad path through trees planted in the 1970s.

Stay on the main path until, forking left, you climb past your first orchids to the Manchester, Bury and Bolton Canal, which opened in 1796. Then turning right, and with extensive views over the Irwell Valley, the cobbled towpath leads to the cottages at Nob End.

Here the short route goes off downhill, but the main walk continues along the now empty canal. There is a high embankment with a precipitous drop into the valley, and then you come to the canal breach. After a warehouse, the next section is maintained by Tonge Angling Club, but a derelict barge lies abandoned beyond, a rusting steam crane remembers former glories, and swans nest among the reeds.

Now with a more open view, continue past the cottages then, immediately after the bridge, a footpath leads out to a track. Follow this down to the road and go right to the footbridge. Crossing the Irwell, keep straight on and up to a junction, following the Irwell Valley Way, then down to join the disused railway.

Turning right along the tree-lined Outwood Cutting, you pass Ringley Road Station and continue under the huge red-brick road bridge. Stay on the line for another quarter of a mile, then a steep flight of steps on the right leads up to a track.

Turn right and, passing the white house, go right again on the tarmac lane. At the bend, a stile leads into the field and you turn left along the edge, down into Ringley Wood. Emerging from the oak trees, go right, just after the house, and the old lane leads into

The giant newt

Ringley with its 1625 Clock Tower, and pack-horse bridge built 50 years later.

Crossing straight over the road, take the footpath through the trees which, after climbing to cross the busy A667, continues through the undergrowth. Then suddenly you are back beside the canal, and this leads high above the Irwell to the aqueduct. There is a fine 18th century pack-horse bridge down to the left, while the canal ends in a pool, where a flight of six locks once climbed to the 'top cut'.

Joining the Short Route, go left through a kissing gate into a flower-rich area. Once this was vat waste from a sulphuric acid works, but now orchids grow here in profusion. Crossing Wilson's Bridge, turn right up the steps. The path descends again to the River Croal and you follow it upstream past Red Rocks before climbing by Darley Delph Quarry. Joining a tarmac track, turn right and back to the Visitor Centre with its magnificent giant newt, carved by chainsaw from a solid block of wood.

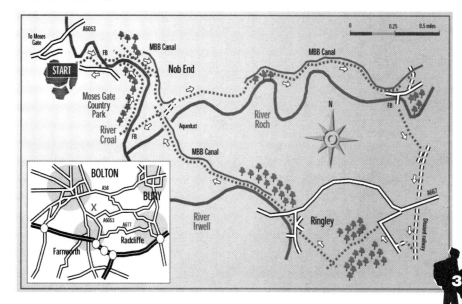

BLOOMIN' DALES

Hartington

LOCATION: 10 miles south east of Buxton

START: Hartington car park, on B5054, toilets

DISTANCE: 6 miles

GRADE: Moderate

TIME: 3 hours

BUS: From Buxton: 442

MAP: Outdoor Leisure - White Peak, Landranger 119

REFRESHMENTS: Hartington

'O my beloved nymph, fair Dove, Princess of rivers, how I love Upon thy flowery banks to lie'. So wrote the 17th century poet, Charles Cotton, and 350 years later the valley is still filled with flowers. Golden rock roses, purple thyme and the nodding heads of musk thistle cover the steep slopes of the dale, while the sparkling River Dove tumbles over little weirs. Then Biggin Dale leads up onto the high plateau, where gleaming limestone walls are a backdrop to the blue-petalled meadow cranesbill. And finally you descend to Hartington, with its cottages grouped around the green, and a hostelry named after the village's most famous son.

THE ROUTE

Leaving Hartington, take the footpath to Dove Dale opposite the car park entrance, behind the toilets. A good path leads over the fields and across a little lane, then descends towards the valley with the tower of Beresford Hall high in the trees ahead. This was the home of Charles Cotton and though the hall is long gone, his 1674 Fishing House, with its pyramid roof, still stands by the riverside.

After a small gate, the surfaced path continues through the trees into Beresford Dale. Large rhubarb-like leaves of butterbur cover the river bank, then a footbridge leads across the Dove by Pike Pool, named not after the fish but the unusual limestone spire. Little weirs break the flow, then a single plank footbridge at Beaver Ford leads back over the river, and the path continues across the field.

Reaching a third footbridge, don't cross but continue beside the Dove into Wolfscote Dale. Frank i'the Rocks cave beckons temptingly, and though not large, it has a polished floor, a chimney, and a very narrow passage leading to a second entrance. With steep slopes and fans of scree sweeping down to the alder trees lining the river, this dale has a completely different character. Sheep are no respecters of flowers, but the rocks are a haven, while beyond the gate there is an abundance of blooms.

Passing the tall pinnacles of Peaseland Rocks, you reach the foot of Biggin Dale. Don't cross the stile but turn left, away from the river. Unlike Dovedale, Biggin Dale is a dry limestone valley, and climbing gently you enter the trees. On the far side of the wall is a trial level dug by miners searching for lead. Rowan and ash have colonised the steep scree slopes, while silverweed, with its silvery pinnate leaves and large buttercup-like flowers, grows on the valley floor.

Entering the Nature Reserve, you emerge into the open and then the dale divides at a signpost by a circular dew pond. Go left through a small gate and follow the

Frank i'th Rocks Cave

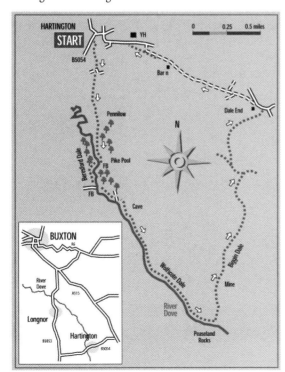

bridleway, keeping straight on up the shallow valley to the road.

Turn left to the cottages at Dale End, then go immediately left up an old pack-horse way. Worn down to the bedrock, this was once used to carry copper ore to Derby for smelting. Taking the right fork, keep straight on at the next junction and over the top of the hill. About 100 yards after a barn, cross a stile in the wall where a path short cuts across the fields to the road.

Turn left past the Jacobean Hartington Hall, the grandest Youth Hostel in the Peak District, where Bonny Prince Charlie slept on his way to London in the 1745 rebellion. Then descending steeply, you are back in Hartington.

BACON BUTTIES & BEER

Climbing away from Gauxholme

LOCATION: 2 miles south of Todmorden

START: Walsden Station (car park on A6033, 50 yards to the south)

DISTANCE: 4 miles

GRADE: Moderate

TIME: 2 hours

TRAIN: Walsden

MAP: Outdoor Leisure - South Pennines, Landranger 103

REFRESHMENTS: Cross Keys Inn

It was hot, the sheep lay panting in the shade and, far below, Todmorden shimmered in the haze as we climbed the old packhorse way. High on the open moor, cows grazed lazily, and a tractor turned the hay in an alpine meadow. Walsden means 'Welsh Valley', but the Celts are long gone, and descending again to the Rochdale Canal we met only friendly Yorkshire folk. Then it was back to the Cross Keys Inn for a relaxing afternoon by the towpath with a bacon butty and a pint. In Walsden, you have a choice of six pubs, but in the good old days there were 20!

THE ROUTE

Opposite Walsden Station, Alma Road leads to the Rochdale Canal where you turn left along the towpath. This waterway, which opened in 1804 to link Manchester with Sowerby Bridge, was the first to cross the Pennines, and passing a couple of locks, a mile post shows a distance of 21 miles from the city centre.

Crossing the main road, where until recently the canal was culverted, the towpath continues on the opposite bank, under the railway, to Gauxholme Highest Lock. Here you leave the canal, and turning left up Bacup Road, with its overhanging rocky cliff, go left again up Naze Road. A bridge leads across Midgelden Brook and, after bending left through a gate, the track zigzags up the hill.

This is the Todmorden Centenary Way Link Path, and beneath the grass are the cobbles of an old packhorse way. It is a steady climb and soon there is a bird's-eye view of the canal, which lies in a gorge formed by glacial melt-water at the end of the Ice Age.

The track passes Law Hey Farm and the ruined Naze Farm, then the angle eases and, after a section flanked by gritstone walls, you emerge onto Inchfield Pasture. Continue by the wall to a signpost and turn left along the farm track, then keep straight on at the bend to follow a 300 year-old causey over the grassy moor.

Continue straight on across Foul Clough Road, which served a mining hamlet in the 1800s, and go through the gate by the houses at Brown Road. The grassy track by Thorns Greece - where even the cattle trough has gold taps - descends into the steep-sided Ramsden Clough, and crossing Ragby Bridge continues up to a signpost. Aiming for the higher signpost, you climb beside the wall to reach a track, then turn left to pass above Inchfield Farm, which dates back to the 15th century.

Joining the tarmac farm road, this leads down through scattered oak trees and between the mill ponds to the Walsden Printing Company. Ramdsen Clough Road continues past a row of terraced handloom weavers' cottages, then you turn left along the main road.

After passing a factory shop and a garden centre, an unsurfaced track on the right, immediately after the railway bridge, leads to the Rochdale Canal

Reflections in the Rochdale Canal

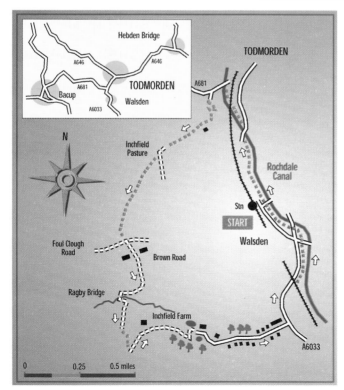

and Winterbutlee Locks. Turn left along the towpath past Nit Square Locks and the rear of the Cross Keys Inn to Travis Mill Locks, where there is a fine view of the 19th century Walsden Church.

Crossing St Peter's Gate, go under a bridge, where the tow ropes have bitten into the stone, then after an old mill you are back at Alma Road and Walsden Station.

SHORE THING FOR SMUGGLERS

LOCATION: Thurstaston, 3 miles north-west of Heswall, toilets

START: Wirral Country Park, signed from A540

DISTANCE: 5 miles (follow the red trail for a 3 mile walk)

GRADE: Moderate

TIME: 3 hours

MAP: Pathfinder 738, Landranger 108

REFRESHMENTS: Cafe near Thurstaston Centre

Heswall Fields

Once the haunt of smugglers who looked down from high sandstone outcrops (with extensive views across the Dee Estuary), the ancient track-ways of Wirral lead across meadows and moorland. Kestrels hover on the wind and flowers line the cliffs above the sandy beach. Here, at the turn of the tide, huge flocks of redshank and oystercatchers feed on the mudflats, while human beachcombers hunt among the polished multi-coloured pebbles for mermaid's purses, whelks egg cases and delicate sea shells.

THE ROUTE

From the car park, go onto the Wirral Way and turn left along the old railway. Although this closed in 1967, due to lack of traffic, there are now probably more walkers than it ever had passengers. Tall spikes of rosebay willowherb flank the track, and soon the horse riders are segregated as the walk follows the blue way-marks along a parallel path.

The shady line continues under the brick arch of Dungeon Bridge which, despite its size, only carried local farm vehicles, then, after a quarter of a mile, you turn left to The Dungeon. This is Old English for a wooded stream, and after a hay meadow the path enters the trees. Crossing the bridge, you climb the steps, then turning right - above a sandstone cave used by smugglers - the path leads past a small waterfall, the only one on the Wirral.

At the top of the wood, turn right along the path known as Oldfield Road, which leads through the fields, with the Wirral's best view of the Dee Estuary and the Clwydian Hills. The path continues past Oldfield Farm, an old manor house which was once moated, then reaching the tarmac, you keep straight on at the junction. Just beyond the former Cleaver Hospital, built as a TB convalescent home for Liverpool children, a footpath on the right leads down to Heswall Dale Nature Reserve.

The track bends left to pass Dale Farm, a horticultural Training Centre, and going left again you keep to the main path, still following the blue way-marks. Crossing the lowland heath, below lie old, red sandstone quarries and beyond is the salt marsh, where cord-grass fills the silted estuary.

Just as the bungalows appear, a way-mark points right, then the path emerges into a housing estate. Keep straight on, turning left on Pipers Lane and right along the main road. This leads down over the railway bridge and round a bend, then just before the shop, originally fishermen's cottages, the disused railway is rejoined.

Turning left towards Thurstaston, follow the track for half a mile until, beyond a couple of wooden barriers, you go left, signed Heswall Fields and Beach. The fenced path leads to a kissing gate and turning right, continues along a field to another kissing gate, and then to a track. Go left beside Heswall Fields, bright with wild carrot, tufted vetch and rest harrow, and down the steps to the beach. (NB. During Spring tides, return along the cliff top.)

Shore Cottages

Turning right, you follow the shore below crumbly red cliffs, which are of glacial drift, a relic of the Ice Age, and some of the embedded boulders come from as far away as Scotland. Tiny pink and white shells, called Thin Tellins, lie scattered on the beach along with the larger, conical Peppery Furrows and also blue Common Mussels.

Reaching the whitewashed Shore Cottages, turn up the steps immediately before the house, where a little path leads through the dell and straight across Station Road to the Thurstaston Centre.

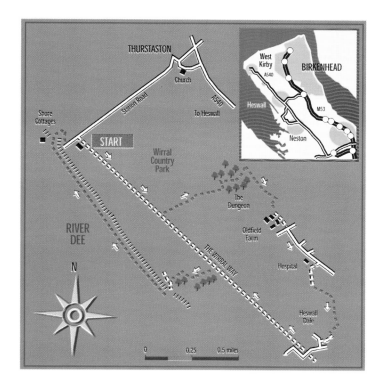

41

THE GRAND TOR

LOCATION: East of Hathersage
START: Turn left off A625, just after the Millstone Inn. Parking in 2 miles by Upper Burbage Bridge
DISTANCE: 4 miles
GRADE: Moderate
TIME: 2½ hours
MAP: Outdoor Leisure - Dark Peak, Landranger 110
REFRESHMENTS: Hathersage

Higger Tor from Carl Wark

Standing on the isolated rocky knoll of Carl Wark, high above Hathersage, it is easy to imagine yourself back 3000 years, for this was an Iron Age fortress. Set in the midst of open moorland, surrounded by steep gritstone slopes and a massive boulder wall, it was a superb defensive position. And from the summit, or from its companion Higger Tor, which means higher, the views stretch for miles. With heather moors, a babbling brook, dramatic gritstone tors and even a little pack-horse bridge, this is the Dark Peak at its very best.

THE ROUTE

From the parking area, just before the road bridge, cross the stile by the Boundary of Open Country Notice and fork right. The path leads away from the stream and, keeping high above the valley, follows Fiddler's Elbow before dipping to climb the steps to Higger Tor. These isolated gritstone knolls were formed when the softer surrounding rock weathered away. Heathery slopes dip to the plantation below, and across the valley is Burbage Moor, while westwards lies the Vale of Edale where a plume of steam marks the 439ft chimney of the Cement Works.

Continue over the rock-strewn top of the tor, with its weirdly eroded boulders and precipitous cliffs. Then, at the far end, you pick your way down through the jumbled boulders and follow the obvious path to the Iron Age hill fort of Carl Wark.

The huge blocks of the defensive wall can clearly be seen, while to the right there is an information plaque and an old stone trough. Beyond lies the original entrance to the fort, where the gritstone wall turns inwards, and on the steep eastern slopes you can find unfinished millstones.

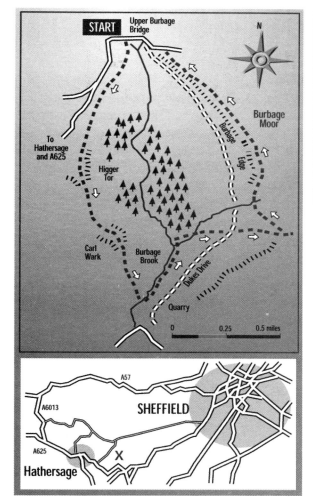

Burbage Edge

Descending either from the original entrance, or from the far end of the knoll, continue in the same direction to join the clear path that leads on down the valley. Burbage Brook is crossed easily by some great stones, then you follow the brook upstream to the pack-horse bridge (if it's very deep, then you can stay on the left bank). With tormentil and cross-leaved heath in flower, these grassy banks make an ideal picnic spot.

From the bridge, thought to be on the line of an old Roman road from the fort at Brough to another in Sheffield, a path leads up beside the plantation. Climbing away from the trees, you fork right and up to meet Duke's Drive, built in the 19th century by the Duke of Rutland who had a shooting lodge at Longshaw. A way-mark points left, then after 50 yards, at another way-mark, you leave the track to follow a path up the shallow side-valley. To the right, standing black against the sky, is a disused quarry, which was used for building stone.

Reaching a large cairn, you turn left, beside a ruined wall, across Burbage Moor. With extensive views across the valley to Carl Wark and Higger Tor, the path follows the edge of the moor, where the green caterpillars of the Emperor Moth feed in summer on the heather. The male adult moths travel great distances and these Romeos can detect a female up to 2km away.

The path continues above Burbage Rocks, but a more interesting route follows the top of the climbing cliffs, and you meet the road again at Upper Burbage Bridge.

WE'RE GOING TO THE CHAPEL

Jenkin Chapel

LOCATION: 4 miles north east of Macclesfield

START: Lamaload Reservoir car park. Follow signs to Saltersford from B5470, then turn right towards Wildboarclough, toilets

DISTANCE: 5½ miles

GRADE: Moderate

TIME: 3 hours

MAP: Outdoor Leisure - White Peak, Landranger 118

REFRESHMENTS: Pack a flask

Looking out over the quiet valley of Todd Brook, on the edge of the Peak District, Jenkin Chapel stands alone. Yet when it was built, over 260 years ago, this was a busy thoroughfare, for the little gritstone building, with its plain whitewashed interior and tall box pews, lay on the medieval saltway from Macclesfield. Once ponies laden with salt crossed the brook at Saltersford, but now it is a backwater, and even on a Bank Holiday you won't meet many other walkers in this secluded corner of the Peak.

THE ROUTE

From the car park, go back onto the road and turn right. With a fine view of the 37-year-old Lamaload Reservoir, you walk down Hooley Hey Lane, then at the bend a stile leads left into the fields. An old track climbs beside the plantation, where marsh thistles grow by the stream, then reaching a solitary gatepost you turn left over a way-marked stile.

Passing the ruined Eaves Farm, head towards Redmoor Farm, and go through the farm yard, then keep straight on across the track. The path bends right and way-marks point across the pasture where, as we passed, the newly-shorn sheep looked almost anorexic without their winter coats. Below lies Todd Brook, but keep above the ruined wall until a pathless, steep descent brings you down to a stile at the bottom of King's Clough. The route now follows the empty valley, staying a little above the stream and, after a shaley bank, a narrow trod soon develops.

After crossing a substantial gritstone wall, the head of the valley comes into view, and fording the stream a track hairpins back below the ruined Thursbitch Farm. Climbing gently, you pass a newly-built stone wall, then leaving the track at the bend, the path continues above Howlersknowl Farm to join the farm track out to the road.

Taking the footpath almost opposite, continue over fields full of harebells and mountain pansies, down to Green Stack. Turn left along the farm track, then leave it at the bend to head directly for Jenkin Chapel. This was built on the site of an ancient cross and the 1842 map shows there was also a school here.

A signpost indicates Rainow and, though there is little sign of the path, you head over Fox Hill and down to the footbridge by the barn. Cross the stile opposite and climb beside the hedgerow to reach a stile where a way-mark points up to the wood. Pausing to look back, the land is laid out like a map, and to the right of the chapel lies Saltersford Farm, which dates back to 1593.

Lamaload Reservoir Dam

The path slants up through the plantation, turning sharp left near the top then, emerging into the open, you keep straight on across the fields. Reaching the road, go left, then at the dip turn right to follow the farm track along Waggonshaw Brow.

A way-marked path goes behind the farm and leads on through a series of stiles, with extensive views over Lamaload Reservoir. Reaching Common Barn, with its turkey sheds, keep straight on, then beyond a large field, you turn left to join the track down past Yearnslow Farm, which means Heron's Hill.

The green lane continues down towards the dam and the waterworks houses, where you turn left up the track. Keep straight on at the bend, heading for a way-mark on the skyline, and back through the plantation to the car park.

GET FELLS IN!

Signpost by Higher Fair Snape

LOCATION: Forest of Bowland
START: 2 miles north-west of Chipping.
Grid reference 602442 on road to Fell Foot,
which starts from the corner by the
entrance to Wolfen Hall Estate
DISTANCE: 5 miles
GRADE: Strenuous
TIME: 3 hours
NOTE: Sorry, no dogs on Fair Snape Fell
(but you can climb Parlick and Wolf Fell,
then return the same way)
MAP: Outdoor Leisure - Forest of Bowland,
Landranger 102
REFRESHMENTS: Pack a flask

With Access Agreements and Concession Paths, the Bowland Fells are gradually being opened up to walkers. Steep grassy slopes rise to Parlick and the wild grouse moors of Fair Snape Fell, while beneath the hillside ancient farmsteads, dating back to medieval times, raise sheep and cattle. But why, with all this land available, are the two houses at Fair Snape crammed so close together? Apparently there was a family quarrel, and one of the brothers built his house in front of the old farm to spoil the view… and it does!

THE ROUTE

Follow the tarmac uphill, with the grassy dome of Parlick ahead. As the road comes to an end at Fell Foot cottage, where a windsock flies for hang-gliders, you continue through the gate. The next bit is an uncompromising head-down plod, straight up the hill, but soon you reach the mound of stones on the summit. Local Catholics gathered here during the Jacobite Rebellion and there is an extensive view to Longridge Fell and Pendle Hill.

After crossing the ladder stile, the fence acts as a guide, dipping towards the whaleback of Fair Snape Fell. Continue beside the wall, then, after passing the stony screes at Nick's Chair, the path veers left, following cairns across the open moor.

Reaching a stile by a gate, you continue over sheep-cropped turf to Paddy's Pole Cairn, the huge pile of stones on the 1575ft summit of Fair Snape Fell. There is a neat, four-bay wind shelter, a whitewashed OS trig point, and an extensive view of the Forest of Bowland, while beyond Morecambe Bay lies the Lake District.

Now retrace your steps for about 100 yards to where a hollow way descends the steep hillside. Zigzagging down to a ladder stile, you leave the Access Area and a grassy footpath continues

The two houses at higher Fair Snape

down to another gate. Head left across the fields, then follow the wall down to reach the farm track. The calves here are a third generation cross, fathered by Benedict, the docile Charolais bull. These animals are named like cars, with an initial letter denoting their age, so this makes him about 10 years old.

Reaching Higher Fair Snape Farm, which was built in 1637, you go straight on through the farmyard and over the stile, then turn left at the signpost. About 50 yards down the tarmac drive, a way-mark points left and you follow the track across the fields. Then, nearing the trees, the right of way crosses a stile to a footbridge over the infant River Brock.

Way-marks point the way up to another stile and then along the fence. After briefly joining a track to cross a stream, you climb to another stile, and continue climbing above Blindhurst Farm, whose name means dark wooded hill. Ignoring the way-mark pointing right, the path follows the old hedgerow across the hillside and back into the Access Area.

Crossing the stile by the next notice, go left to the field corner. Way-marks point on across the slopes of Parlick and a stone staircase leads over the wall: keeping straight on, you continue over more stiles back to the Fell Foot road junction.

47

THE CORK & CAT WALK

LOCATION: Peak District, 5 miles south-east of Bakewell
START: Birchover, signed from B5056 off A6. Park on Main Street, toilets
DISTANCE: 3 miles
GRADE: Easy
TIME: 2 hours
BUS: From Bakewell 172 (Mon-Sat)
MAP: Outdoor Leisure - White Peak, Landranger 119
REFRESHMENTS: Druid Inn

Nine ladies stone circle

Stanton Moor is a little gem. Set amidst encircling White Peak limestone, this isolated, heathery plateau is crammed full of Bronze Age burial mounds and stone circles. The Nine Ladies Circle was built 4000 years ago, and legend says these are the figures of nine maidens turned to stone for their pagan dancing. The Cork Stone, though, is natural and the ascent, using its iron rings and footholds, is a must. In late summer, with acres of honey-scented heather and juicy, finger-staining bilberries, this is one of our favourite walks.

THE ROUTE

Start by walking up Birchover's Main Street, past the end of Uppertown Lane and by the Pinfold, where stray animals were once kept. Then, as the houses come to an end, you fork right, opposite the stone works, along the track to Barn Farm.

Passing through the camp site, a signpost beyond the farm indicates left and you go round the back of the buildings and past Sabinehay Barn to where a way-mark points up the edge of the field. Reaching the lane, go right and in a few steps a stile leads onto Stanton Moor.

The sandy path climbs through the bracken, until at the junction, you fork right to head towards a prominent boulder. Crossing a stile, by the National Trust sign, the route then follows the fence along Stanton Moor Edge. The ruins of a small quarry are passed (beware of steep drops hereabouts!) and you look down on Darley Dale, while in the distance the twin towers of Riber Castle stand silhouetted against the sky.

The path dips, and just off to the right is the Cat Stone, an isolated gritstone tor whose carved footholds and inscription 'EIN 1831' were the work of the Thornhill family of Stanton Hall.

As the heather gives way to bracken, you enter the trees, then suddenly the tower appears. It commemorates that landmark in democracy, Earl Grey's 1832 Reform Bill. Here you cross the stile and, turning right, the path leads through the bracken heading straight for the Nine Ladies Stone Circle. This lies on the far side of the main track and the King Stone, the petrified figure of the high priest, is a little beyond.

Returning to the broad path, you turn right, and follow it across the moor past South Circle, a large earth ring. Over 70 burial mounds lie scattered on the moor, all of which were excavated in the 1930s by the Heathcotes, who had a private museum in Birchover.

Just before the path junction, there are the remains of a tumulus, the largest on the moor, which contained 13 burials. Then, turning right, you continue to the Cork Stone. In the 18th century, this isolated boulder, which has 'WWM 1864' carved under the overhang, was surrounded by four standing stones.

Keep straight on, and the path leads out to the road where you turn left. Reaching Ann Twyford Stone Quarry, which still has the machinery for making millstones, turn right through the visitor's car park. On the far side, there is a fine view across the valley to Youlgreave, and a narrow path sets off downhill

John climbing the cork stone

through the trees. Passing piles of huge blocks from an old quarry, it seems a long way down, then suddenly the path emerges onto the road by the Druid Inn, and you are back in Birchover.

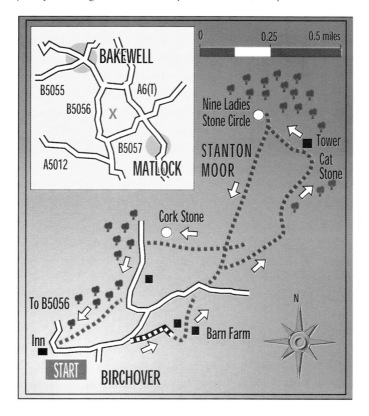

LOCKS AND QUAYS

LOCATION: 5 miles west of Northwich
START: Crewood Common Rd, off B5153
between Acton Bridge & Kingsley. Park in ¾
mile, just before the cottages
DISTANCE: 3½ miles
GRADE: Easy
TIME: 1½ hours
MAP: Pathfinder 757, Landranger 117
REFRESHMENTS: Pack a flask

Lower Dutton Horse Bridge

Hijacking is not a common occurence in Cheshire nowadays, but in the 1730s they stole a whole river. Once, the Weaver flowed in slow, meandering loops across the countryside, but then came the salt trade, and the engineers didn't do things by halves. Widened, deepened and straightened, the Weaver Navigation became one of the North West's busiest waterways, and Dutton Locks was built on a massive scale. Things are much quieter now, and if you are lucky enough to see an ocean-going vessel, it feels as if you have stepped back in time.

THE ROUTE

Take the road opposite the house with the owls on the gateposts. Then, at the T-junction, turn left along Ainsworth Lane, to pass a fine red-brick 19th century barn. Opposite Poplar Farm, which was rebuilt in 1881, a signpost points left through a gate, and a way-marked path leads straight on by the hedge, and beside a line of oaks.

Turning sharp right over Cliff Brook, climb the flight of steps onto the hilltop, and continue to a stile at the end of an old green lane. The grassy track, edged with purple tufted vetch and the tall pink spikes of rosebay willowherb, bends left to join Cliff Lane, where you turn right and under the railway bridge.

Reaching the road junction go left, towards Dutton, past the tall gables of Weaver Holt. This is the route of the Delamere Way, a 20 mile long-distance footpath, way-marked by a yellow arrow with a green dot.

At the imposing Manor Farm, you continue through the gate and down the track, with extensive views over the Weaver Valley. As the track ends, a way-mark points left, then going over a stile the path follows the hedge through a field bright with the golden stars of common ragwort. Though the flowers are very attractive its leaves are poisonous to cattle.

Then suddenly you arrive at Dutton Locks. With its massive twin lock, built to take a 1000 ton coaster, the Navigation linked the canal at Northwich to the River Mersey. A row of lock-keepers' cottages stands by the water, and a sign in four languages is aimed at boats from foreign ports, but on our visit the only vessel in sight was the rusting hulk of the Chica, which once ferried day-trippers.

The wreck of Chica

Turning left along the bank, the route stays on this side of the Weaver Navigation, where marsh woundwort, water mint, water cress and water forget-me-not flourish among the reeds. Passing the white, twin-arched Lower Dutton Horse Bridge, which was built in 1919 over a section of the old river, you go under the spectacular 19th century Dutton Viaduct and by the ICI pumping station. A meander of the old River Weaver, bypassed by Pickerings Cut, lies abandoned and forgotten, save by the coots, which are easily identified by their white foreheads and bills.

Now the footpath turns away from the water near the site of Pickerings Wharf. Before 1732, and the building of the Navigation, salt was brought here by packhorses and loaded onto boats which took it out to the sea.

Then reaching the road end, you follow the tarmac uphill, past the houses at Pickerings, and straight on at the junction back to the start.

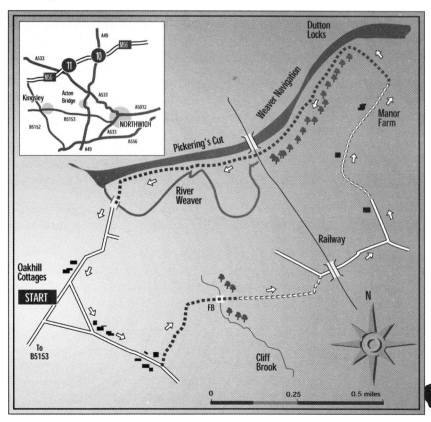

WILD COUNTRY OF THE LONE RANGER

Butterley reservoir and Pule hill

LOCATION: 7 miles west of Huddersfield

START: Marsden Station, roadside parking

DISTANCE: Five miles

GRADE: Moderate

TIME: 2½ hours

BUS: From Oldham 365

TRAIN: Marsden

MAP: Outdoor Leisure - South Pennines, Landranger 110

REFRESHMENTS: Marsden

Mention the National Trust and everyone immediately thinks of grand, stately homes, but they also own vast acres of mountains and moorland. Marsden Moor, near Huddersfield, is one of their estates, a typical high Pennine grassland with golden plover, grouse and curlew. Here, seated in the warm sunshine among the tumbled stones of a ruined farm, Malcolm, a volunteer ranger, talked of tunnels under Pule Hill, and of Roman roads and ancient routes across the Pennines, while above us a kestrel hovered in the wind.

THE ROUTE

From Marsden Station, walk down Station Road, then turn right over the River Colne and up Peel Street, with its imposing clock tower atop the Mechanics Institute. Crossing Manchester Road, you go through the park, heading for the bandstand and the memorial to Sam Laycock, the local dialect poet, who wrote 'Welcome, Bonny Brid'.

A little gate leads out onto the road and, taking the lane almost opposite, you climb past the weavers' cottages. Then, at the bend, keep straight on and follow the footpath up the field to Scout Farm. A few yards left along the sandy track there is a stile, by the NT notice, onto the 5685 acre Marsden Moor Estate.

Climbing on, with the view of Marsden in the valley below, you join a grassy track and turn left. Then on meeting a main track, turn sharply right and continue up to cross Blackmoorfoot Conduit, which feeds the reservoir near Huddersfield.

Reaching Deer Hill Conduit, beneath the disused Shooters Nab Quarries, you turn right beside the water channel, which soon is dry, for the water is now piped from Wessenden Head Reservoir. A couple of little stone bridges span the channel above the isolated farm at Upper Acre Head, then rounding the bend, Butterley Reservoir comes into view.

Beyond lie the steep slopes of Pule Hill, a major obstacle which road builders have tackled in several different ways. There is Mount Road, and above it the old road, while higher up you can just make out a grassy ledge, thought to be the line of the Roman road from Slack to Castleshaw. The modern A62 takes the easier route round the back, then all join up to cross Standedge at the notch on the skyline.

Crossing the head of Rams Clough, where an old sluice gate stands forlorn, continue to the next bridge. Here you leave the catch-water path and, after a brief scramble down over tussocky grass to the wall, this is followed past a ruined farm to a grand bridge, restored by the NT.

The path leads up to the lane end, but turn off immediately, down to the wall and follow this to a stile. A very narrow path, which can be slippery, leads downhill into the Wessenden Valley, and keeping left you continue down to the track. Turn right, beside Butterley Reservoir, which was built about 1907, then reaching the road, you go left and through a green gate.

A flight of 205 steps leads down past an isolated gritstone tenter post, used for stretching cloth from the mills. Keep right, along the track and through the buildings of Bank Bottom Mill. Continue down Binn Road and Fall Lane, and under the A62, then passing the parish church and the memorial to Enoch Taylor, the inventor of the Cropping Frame, a sort of textile lawn mower, you are back at Station Road.

Sluice Gate by Rams Clough

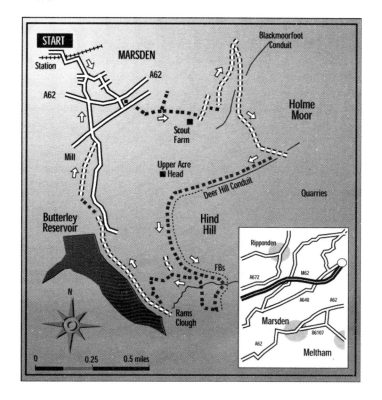

A MASS OF MASTS

LOCATION: 4 miles north of Rawtenstall
START: Clowbridge Reservoir on A682. Park by track beneath the dam
DISTANCE: 5 miles
GRADE: Moderate
TIME: 3 hours
BUS: X43
MAP: Outdoor Leisure - South Pennines, Landranger 103
REFRESHMENTS: Pack a flask

Golf ball on Hameldon Hill

Sprouting like giant trees, high above the Burnley Road, the wireless masts on Hameldon Hill are a landmark for miles around. But Hamel means treeless and it is well named for the hill is bare, with steep, grassy slopes sweeping down to the site of a medieval settlement. Gambleside was abandoned when Clowbridge Reservoir was built, and little sign remains of its seven collieries. Now the fields have reverted to moorland, while sailing boats tack to and fro and windsurfers capsize spectacularly in a plume of spray.

THE ROUTE

From the parking area, continue up the sailing club track and fork right at the Gambleside Trail notice to a stile by a gate. Turning right, with the masts on Hameldon Hill ahead, the wide path leads to the main road, which was turnpiked in 1795. Go left, then, after Alma Terrace, a footpath on the right follows a raised bank across the field.

Go left through the farm gate, and right past Dunnockshaw Farm. Leaving the track, you descend to a footbridge over Limy Water, whose name refers to the lime carried here by pack-horses from Clitheroe.

Straight ahead is a stile, and entering the plantation, a path climbs through the trees to join a grassy ride. Turn left and follow it uphill until, at the bend, you go left to a stile out onto a fire break. Crossing another stile, the path continues up through the wood, staying near the edge, to reach a stile out into the open.

Now veering away from the trees, you climb on across the moor, with an aerial view of Love Clough village. Love means watery and there is still plenty of water to be seen in the old mill lodges. After passing through a gateway, a faint path leads up to the head of Whin Hill Clough and the arched entrance of an old lead mine.

The next bit is rather rough, but it doesn't last long, and after following the fence up to a stile you turn left along a track. Darwen Tower appears on the distant skyline, and below is Great Clough where coal was mined from 1820. Then reaching a gate, you turn right along the 40 mile-long Burnley Way, which leads easily past the four tall wireless masts and the white golf ball of the Radar Weather Station.

Joining the tarmac, follow it down to a cattle grid then, a few yards beyond, an indistinct path to the left goes downhill, parallel to the road. Reaching New Laithe, the tarmac is rejoined for about half a mile, before the Burnley Way continues along the hillside behind the white houses. These were built in the middle of the last century when the mines were busy.

Passing an old quarry, the track leads to a gate, but heading up to a yellow-topped post, the way continues through the site of an old colliery to join Tom Fort's Lane at Higher Nutshaw. Climbing on, there are good views of Clowbridge Reservoir and, after an unfenced section, the lane arrives at Manchester Road.

Turn right, then, in about 300 yards, an unsurfaced track leads across an arm of the reservoir. This is where the ancient hollow-way of Limers Gate, which linked the Ribble Valley with Rochdale, was cut off when the

Windsurfers on Clowbridge Reservior

valley was flooded in 1866. A concession path then follows the reservoir edge past the site of Gambleside Colliery back to the Sailing Clubhouse and the dam.

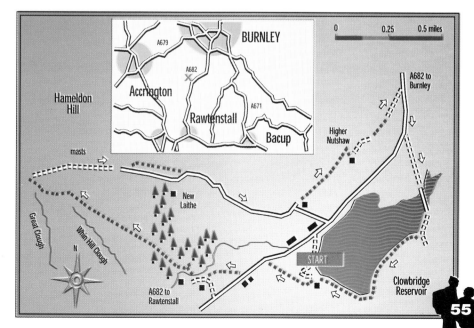

MOOS

Through the trees on Lindow Common

LOCATION: Wilmslow
START: Car park on Racecourse Road, off A538, opposite Boddington Arms
DISTANCE: 4 miles
GRADE: Easy
TIME: 2 hours
TRAIN: Wilmslow (1 mile)
BUS: 130
MAP: Pathfinder 741, Landranger 109
REFRESHMENTS: Yates Garden Centre & Boddington Arms

'Body found in bog!' ran the headlines. But the police quickly lost interest when the corpse found buried on Lindow Moss, near Wilmslow, turned out to be 2000 years old. It was a sacrifice to water gods, and there is still plenty of water here, including a brand-new lake edged with 'brandy bottle' water-lilies. Though named from the shape of the seed heads, the flowers also smell of alcohol, which explains the satisfied smile of the cow, slurping away up to its neck in the water.

THE ROUTE

A kissing gate at the back of the car park leads onto Lindow Common and you follow the main path through the silver birch trees. Keep straight on at the junction, across the heather, and continue in the same direction to reach Black Lake. This was restored in 1986 using a clay liner, much to the delight of the swans and gulls.

Go round to the left, by the water's edge until, just after rounding the far end of the lake, a narrow path diverges onto the scrubby heath. Follow this across another path and continue to a four-way junction where you turn left, out to Racecourse Road. In the 19th century, this was indeed used for horse racing.

Crossing straight over, go down Lindow Lane for about 50 yards, then turn left through the gates of Bramford. The bridleway leads past the house and continues round the edge of the woodland. Emerging onto another bridleway, go left and continue to a T-junction where you turn right along a track on the fringe of the wood. It's then left at the next junction and left again onto Rotherwood Road, a wide track.

Reaching the houses at Stormy Point, the unsurfaced road is more attractive, so take the second turning right and follow Leigh Road to Hetlee Farm, dated 1907. The footpath continues to Studholme Kennels, where you go right for a few yards, then left along Moor Lane, past the Garden Centre (and coffee shop!).

Fork right at the next junction and, with the white trumpets of convolvulus entwined in the hedge, the tarmac lane leads past the Peat Depot to the entrance to Lindow Court. The footpath is signed right, then in 50 yards, you turn right again to cross the tarmac track onto Lindow Moss. Peat is being extracted here, and in 1983 a female skull was dug up, causing a local man to confess to the murder of his wife. The corpse turned out to be Roman, and in the following year they found Lindow Man, who is now in the British Museum.

Cow up to it's neck

After crossing the narrow-gauge railway, and its two attendant footbridges, head slightly left to reach another footbridge, where way-marks indicate the route through a Nature Reserve. Then reaching the track by Saltersley Hall, you turn right past Rossmere, created by sand quarrying when constructing the M56.

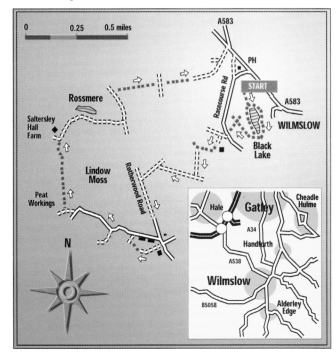

The track skirts the edge of the fishing lake and leads out to Rotherwood Road again. Turning left towards Morley, follow the track down into the dip, then as the tarmac comes to an end, go right along the bridleway. Crossing straight over a rough track, continue through woodland and past the allotments, then the lane bends left to the A538. Follow the main road into Wilmslow for just a few yards, then turn right down an unsurfaced track which leads back to the Boddington Arms.

HAUNTED BY THE LOST LAD

Rocks at Back Tor

LOCATION: 10 miles east of Glossop

START: Derwent Valley, signed from A57. Fairholmes car park, toilets

DISTANCE: 7 (or 5) miles

GRADE: Strenuous

TIME: 4 hours

MAP: Outdoor Leisure - Dark Peak, Landranger 110

REFRESHMENTS: Kiosk at Fairholmes

Surrounded by pinewoods, and with their blue waters fringed with beech trees, the reservoirs of the Upper Derwent are in a delightful setting. They are popular, too, with people hoping for a glimpse of the villages drowned when the valley was flooded. But as you climb the steep slopes that lead up to the wind-eroded rocks of Back Tor, the crowds are soon left behind. Perched by the whitewashed trig point, the view stretches towards Bleaklow, and you feel the call of the wilderness beyond.

THE ROUTE

From Fairholmes Visitor Centre, a footpath leads through the trees to Derwent Dam with its Gothic, fairytale towers. The reservoir and this 115ft retaining wall were completed in 1916 after 15 years work.

Abandoning the tarmac road, head across the grass and up the steps to the right, then reaching the top you turn left on a broad track beside the 176 acre reservoir. In about half a mile, a green footpath notice marks the start of a path that climbs through the trees to reach the open hillside. Ascending steeply, the way-marked route zigzags up through the bracken, and soon you are high above the reservoir. Photographers here have an advantage, disguising rests by frequent stops to capture the view over the Upper Derwent Valley to the distant patchwork heather moors.

At last the angle eases, and passing a signpost you keep straight on and follow the ruined wall across the moor. To the north, Margery Hill comes into view with Howden Edge and Grinah Stones beyond, while to the south lie Kinder and the Mam Tor ridge.

Arriving at another signpost by a stile, designed specially for dogs and people with short legs, you continue in the same direction along the grassy track. A broader track is soon joined and here the Shorter Route turns back.

The long walk continues, following the main track up towards the high ground beside a ditch marking the Sheffield City Boundary. Then, ascending more steeply, the path climbs to the Sheffield Clarion Ramblers topograph on Lost Lad. Here, in the 16th century, the body of a shepherd boy missing in a blizzard was found with the words 'Lost Lad' scratched on a rock beside him.

Slabs of stone from old mills lead on to Back Tor, the ultimate objective. This must be the most difficult to reach trig point in the Peak, but standing at 1765 feet you are rewarded for your efforts by a spectacular moorland panorama.

The return route now follows the flagged path along Derwent Edge for about 300 yards to a prominent

Back Tor

upright marker stone, at Bradfield Gate Head, where you turn right. The old footpath from Strines leads down through the heather, then in about a mile the outward route is briefly rejoined. Forking left and left again, a track crosses the moor to join another track at a signpost. Turning left, this follows the wall over Pike Low, with its ancient tumulus, and ahead lies the arched Ladybower Viaduct, then veering left you leave the Open Country.

Descending past Lanehead Farm, an old sunken lane descends to the road. Turning right past St Henry's School, built for Roman Catholic children but now the community hall, you reach Old House Farm. This stood on the outskirts of Derwent Village, which disappeared under the water when the valley was flooded in the mid-1940s. Then forking left, down to Derwent Dam, you are soon back at the start of the walk.

ON THE BEACON TRACK

Bolton Bridge

LOCATION: 6 miles east of Skipton

START: Lay-by on B6160, just south of A59 roundabout at Bolton Bridge

DISTANCE: 7 miles

GRADE: Moderate

TIME: 4 hours

MAP: Explorer - Lower Wharfedale, Landranger 104

REFRESHMENTS: Pack a flask

Standing high above Wharfedale, Beamsley Beacon is the southernmost hill of the Yorkshire Dales National Park. It is a magnificent viewpoint, and after climbing the heather-clad slopes you look out from the pointed cairn at a full skyline of moorland. Far below, the River Wharfe meanders through the meadows and past an ancient mill. Herons flap lazily across the water, while on the grassy banks Friesian cattle and Dales-bred sheep gaze placidly at laden backpackers tramping along the Dales Way.

THE ROUTE

From the lay-by, walk towards the roundabout, and turn right through a little gate. The path leads under the new road bridge, built in 1993, and across a field to the old ferry house. Turning right over the medieval Bolton Bridge, which was originally made of wood, you follow the lane past Red Lion Farm and out to join the A59.

Fortunately it's only a short way on the busy road before a quiet lane leads right, signed to Beamsley. Then, reaching the first farm, which has a splendid white dovecote, you go left up the track. Crossing a stile by a gate, the footpath follows the old watermill leat, and continues over the field to a stone stepstile in the far corner.

Though there is little sign of a path, stay beside Kex Beck until, climbing out of the valley, Beamsley Beacon comes into view. Reaching the houses of Deerstones, named after the boulders where native red deer rubbed velvet from their antlers, fork right immediately after the gate. A narrow path zigzags down to a footbridge, then a grassy track leads up the far side and continues to the signpost by Ling Chapel Farm.

Turn right along the farm track for 50 yards, then take the grassy trod slanting left across the moor. Briefly joining the tarmac road, where we stopped to admire a splendid 1928 Austin Seven, a signposted path climbs beside the enclosure wall to join the ridge.

It's an 'out and back' to visit the Beacon, but a good path leads along the edge of the grouse moor to the trigpoint, which is dwarfed by a massive cairn. The whole of the Bolton Estate is on show to the north, while to the south lies the long ridge of Ilkley Moor. Strictly this is not the summit, for The Old Pike, a quarter of a mile beyond, is the highest point on the moor.

After returning along the ridge, go between the houses and turn left. Follow the road downhill for ½ mile then, just beyond a farm, turn right by a cattle grid to continue down an old green lane. Gradually, the way narrows and deepens until you look at the cows from hoof level, then emerging into a field, you descend to a lane. Keep straight on, along the track to West Hall, where a tarmac footpath on the right leads to the impressive Suspension Bridge.

Crossing the Wharfe, turn upstream and follow the Dales Way through the trees. Staying by the river, this leads to High Mill, now converted into cottages, then going through the caravan park you continue for a good mile beside the river through fields that

Beamsley Beacon

once were part of a Deer Park. Emerging onto the B6160, turn left, then right, up the drive of Farfield Farm. In a few yards, a stile leads right into the fields where a new concession path hugs the wall for half a mile. Then, rejoining the road, there is a pavement back to the lay-by.

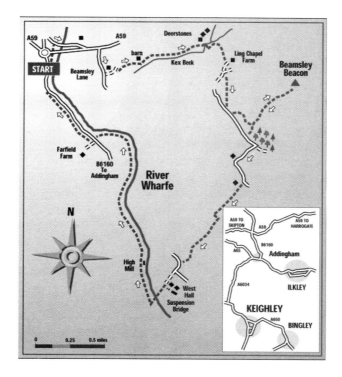

DUTCH DOUBLE

LOCATION: 6 miles west of Chorley
START: B5247, Croston station car park
DISTANCE: 5 miles
GRADE: Easy
TIME: 2½ hours
BUS: From Chorley C7 (not Sun)
TRAIN: Croston
MAP: Pathfinder 699, Landranger 108
REFRESHMENTS: Croston

Cyclist crossing Red Bridge

With its 900-year-old church, pack-horse bridge, ancient school and narrow cobbled street, Croston is one of the most attractive old villages in Lancashire. Yet beneath this tranquil exterior lurks the River Yarrow. Only a few feet above sea level, Croston for centuries suffered from terrible floods. Then, in the 1800s the rivers Lostock and Douglas were straightened and the mosses drained. And now, as you walk along the high embankments, the countryside only needs a few windmills to turn it into Holland.

THE ROUTE

Turning left up Station Road, follow it across the railway and continue along the B5247 for about a quarter of a mile. Then, reaching Lostock Bridge, you turn left along the high flood bank, beside the canalised River Lostock. The insignificant-looking stream seems incapable of misbehaving, and the footpath follows the top of the high embankment through vast, prairie-like fields, where a few hedges remain like groynes on a beach.

All around are huge, empty skies, with only Tarleton church spire breaking the horizon: then, after nearly a mile, the River Yarrow joins to swell the flow. Gradually the nature of the stream changes, with mudflats exposed at low tide, until reaching the River Douglas you turn left along Eyes Lane. The name comes from the many little eyes or islands that were here before the West Lancashire Plain was drained a couple of centuries ago.

This is the route of the 300 mile Lancashire Cycle Way, and you cross the Bailey Bridge, erected in 1985 and confusingly called Red Bridge, though careful inspection shows it was once painted green. Going left again, you walk beside the tidal river, where mallards patrol with a proprietorial air, while in the distance beyond Croston Church is Anglezarke Moor.

At the triple-arched Great Hanging Bridge turn left (watch for cars), then go right on the tarmac track. After a concrete bridge, take the left fork along Finney Lane which leads, straight as a Roman road, to Finney Lane Farm, and over the level crossing. The tarmac lane then comes to a T-junction where you turn left down Moss Lane.

At the bend, just before the craft centre, keep straight on, taking the footpath which crosses a little footbridge and continues across the fields to Back Drinkhouse Lane. Turning left to pass the Jubilee Almshouses, you then go right on Shevington Causeway, past more almshouses erected in 1809.

High concrete flood fences conceal the Yarrow, in its deep channel, and staying by the river you follow Carvers Brow. Don't cross the bridge at Castle Walk, once the site of a wooden fortification, but take the footpath to the right.

Reaching the road turn left, then go right in front of Manor House Farm and left by Manor House Barn into the cemetery. A footpath leads across the river and continues through the archway of the 17th century school, which was founded in 1392. The three schools in Croston have been amalgamated and there are plans for this beautiful building to become a Heritage Centre.

River Yarrow in Croston

After admiring Croston Church, walk up the cobbled Church Street, which has remained unchanged since the 18th century, while the Preaching Cross dates back to 651AD. Turning left on the main road, you pass the medieval pack-horse bridge, the village green and the tea room. Then going straight on at the junction, by the Town Hall and past the 1692 Almshouses, Station Road leads back to the start.

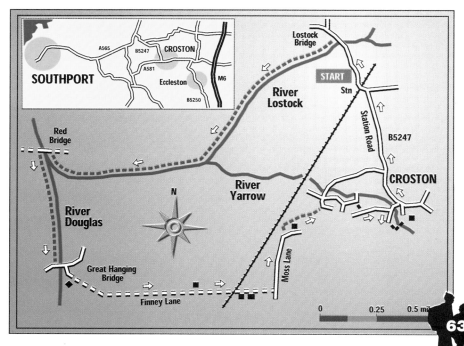

VIEW THAT WON'T GO TO WASTE

Sign at Hard Times Farm

LOCATION: 4 miles east of Hyde
START: Hollingworth. Turn off A57 by the Gun Inn, up Wedneshough Green, and park near Albion Mill
DISTANCE: 4½ miles
GRADE: Moderate
TIME: 2 hours
BUS: 237
MAP: Outdoor Leisure - Dark Peak, Landranger 109 & 110
REFRESHMENTS: Hollingworth

Longdendale wasta est. No, the walk isn't in Latin, but wasteland, worth just 40 shillings, is how the Domesday Book describes the Etherow Valley. Things have looked up since then, with stately gritstone farms on the hillside above Hollingworth. Here William de Peveril, William the Conqueror's illegitimate son, built his hunting lodge in the Royal Forest of the Peak. And the woods are the highlight, for trees in autumn are always a treat, while the extensive views of Longdendale are too good to miss.

THE ROUTE
From the old Albion cotton mill, walk back to the corner where a footpath leads between the attractive 18th century cottages of Wedneshough Green. Emerging into the open, you turn immediately uphill on the footpath which climbs beside the boundary of Longdendale High School.

Mottram Church, once called the Cathedral of East Cheshire, appears high above the valley, then reaching the topmost playing field, you go right to join the sunken Lumb Lane. Turning left, the climb continues up this old packhorse way until, arriving at a T-junction by Lumb Cottage, you turn right. Now the view opens out, with the great trough of Longdendale carving its way between Bleaklow and the northern moors, while opposite lie Kinder and Coombes Edge.

Passing Hard Times Farm (a name surely from Dickens!) and Higher Landslow Green Farm, which lay derelict for ten years, you turn right along Hobson Moor Road. The track continues past the farms of Landslow Green, which date back to the 16th century, and keeping straight on, the tarmac drive leads to Hollingworth Hall Farm.

Hollingworth means the enclosure in the holly, but the gates, alas, are all that remain of the hall. Rebuilt in the 15th century, and housing troops during the Civil War, it was demolished in the 1940s. Passing North West Water's picnic area and restaurant, the track climbs slowly through some fine beech trees. Arnfield and Bottoms Reservoirs come into view and, staying by the wall, you continue across the lower slopes of Hollingworth Moor.

Reaching a stile by a gate, the track begins to descend then, just before the trees that hide the ruins of Middle Bank, you turn back on a grassy track across the hillside. This is the

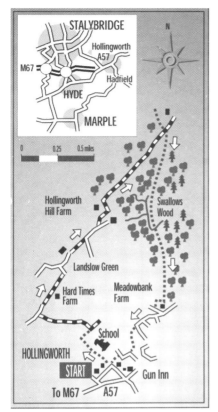

route of the Tameside Trail and way-marks point past the remains of Lower Bank. After traversing the slope below a beech wood, a legacy of the Hollingworth Estate, you descend beside an old hawthorn hedge to enter Swallows Wood.

The path leads gently downhill until, leaving the trees (which are under threat from a new bypass), it continues across the open hill slope. Passing above the dam of the former Hollingworth Reservoir, which was built in 1855 and demolished in 1987 to make a Nature Reserve, the path briefly re-enters the trees. After following the edge of a field, you come to Meadowbank Farm, where way-marks point round to the right of the barn and out onto the road.

Turn right and follow the road until, just after the bend, a track leads down to some cottages. Go left across the field to a stile and continue between a high fence and hedge. Emerging by the old weavers' cottages at Thornecliffe Wood, you take the little cobbled path to the right and keep straight on past the burnt-down chapel and the High School, back to the start of the walk.

Hollingworth Hall Farm

TAKE THE HIGH ROAD

Cyclist on Rooley Moor Road

LOCATION: 4 miles north of Rochdale

START: Whitworth Water Ski Centre, signed from A671 down Tong Lane. Parking at end of Cowm Reservoir dam

DISTANCE: 5½ miles

GRADE: Moderate, but with some rough moorland walking

TIME: 3 hours

BUS: From Rochdale: 464

MAP: Outdoor Leisure - South Pennines, Landranger 109

REFRESHMENTS: Pack a flask

Out on the high moors above Rochdale, it feels like the middle of nowhere, then suddenly you come to a road. But this is no ordinary track, for the Cotton Famine Road is a magnificent cobbled highway. Built to provide work for hard-pressed mill-workers during the American Civil War, when the cotton ports were blockaded, its wheel-worn slabs and close-set stones are a superb piece of engineering, while the setting is both wild and beautiful.

THE ROUTE

The walk starts along the 1875 dam and continues round beside Cowm Reservoir. Though the water looks delightful, it is no longer drinkable since disastrous tyre burning in the Britannia Quarries above polluted the supply.

When a gate is reached across the track, you turn left, through an old wooden gate, and bear right over the field. Crossing the ancient track of Cowclough Lane, a faint path then climbs straight up the hillside, heading for the end of the spoil tips on the skyline.

It's a steep climb, but soon the disused Thurns Head Quarry is reached, where you turn right along an old grassy tramway. This makes for easy walking round the edge of the moor to the quarries on Ragstone Brow. Then, after a fence, the tramway continues along a rocky shelf, high above Walstead Clough.

Reaching the head of the deep ravine, cross the stile and turn left to follow a narrow trod above the stream. Now you are up on the bleak moor, but the wall acts as guide, and the going is not too bad through the tall purple moor-grass. Pity the poor sheep on the heavily grazed far side who must surely have webbed feet.

Just when it seems you are miles from anywhere, grass covered mounds mark the site of Old Sink Slack colliery, and beyond are the grooved causey stones of Rooley Moor Road. Turning left you follow the track, which is now the route of the Rossendale Way, and soon it becomes cobbled. This is the Cotton Famine Road and, passing the track to the extensive Ding Quarry, the Naden Valley reservoirs appear, dominated by the bulk of Knowl Hill, while opposite

Cobbles on the Cotton Famine Road

two huge gate posts are the ruins of the Moorcock Inn, which closed in the 1940s.

Reaching the dip, with Top of Pike cairn ahead, you turn left along a narrower track. There are fine views over the Whitworth Valley, then, after a quarter of a mile, a faint path goes right to a ladder stile. Crossing the stream, the way follows the lip of the disused Bagden Quarry, where roofing and paving slabs still await collection.

At the far end of the quarry, way-marks point down the steep, grassy hillside to a stile and the path continues above the gorge of Fern Isle Wood. Then, descending more steeply towards Spring Mill Reservoir, which still supplies one of the valley's oldest working mills, you cross the footbridge.

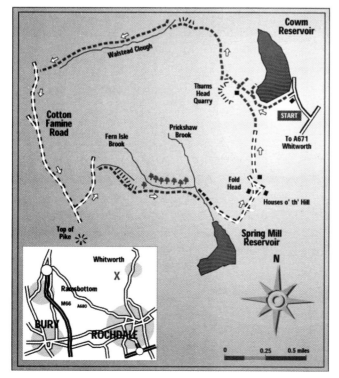

Turn right and climb the track beside the Waterworks wall to Houses o' th' Hill and follow the lane down to the cottages at Fold Head. Keep straight on, staying on the level, and a footpath is joined beside the last house. The way then continues through a deep cutting to the old quarries where a sunken lane leads down the hill back to Cowm Reservoir.

GOING TO THE DOGS

Lud's Church

LOCATION: 6 miles south of Macclesfield

START: Wincle, off A54. Roadside parking beyond the Ship Inn at Danebridge

DISTANCE: 4½ miles

GRADE: Moderate

TIME: 2½ hours

MAP: Outdoor Leisure - White Peak, Landranger 118

REFRESHMENTS: Ship Inn

The great rift of Lud's Church is an eerie place. Surrounded by ferns and mosses, and enclosed between vertical walls, you descend the steps into a shadowy chasm. This is the legendary Green Chapel where, according to a medieval poem, Sir Gawain came to challenge the mysterious Green Knight. Then, climbing to the airy ridge high above, an easy stroll leads to the Hanging Stone with its memorial to Burke. 'A Noble Mastiff, Black and Tan, Faithful as woman, Braver than man, A gun and a ramble, His heart's desire, With the friend of his life, The Swythamley Squire.'

THE ROUTE

Follow the road over the bridge and take the footpath on the left, signed to Gradbach. This leads down to the river and on across a field to climb to a stile into the wood. The path then wanders on through the larches and pines until, emerging into the open, you come to the Scout's cottage at Back Dane with its unexpected view of Shutlingsloe.

After a few yards along the track, the footpath continues across the open hillside, high above the river. Then, passing another isolated cottage, that has been much modernised, you descend to a stile into the Roaches Estate, bought by the Peak Park Board in 1980.

The Dane, which rises on Axe Edge Moor, now flows in a deep gorge with high gritstone cliffs and the path ambles on for another mile through the oaks, silver birch and rowan of Back Forest. After climbing by some tall Scots Pines, a signpost is reached and you turn sharp right to follow the path slanting back up the hillside.

It is a steady climb until, bending left, the path comes to the outcrop of Castle Rocks. This is where people study their maps and ask others the way to Lud's Church, for despite the signposts it keeps its secret well. Take the topmost path on the left, and in 300 yards, you come to the entrance. Lud's Church is named after Walter de Ludauk, leader of the persecuted Lollards who worshipped here in the 14th century. Entering the deep cleft, which is a natural ravine caused by a landslip, steps lead down into the gloomy depths.

At the far end, more steps lead up into daylight and a little path continues along the hillside to a signpost where you turn right up the concession path. As the narrow trod climbs through the heather, the view opens out over the Dane Valley, then reaching the ridge you turn right over a stile. Now the path follows the rocky crest of the hill, while ahead is the scarp silhouette of The Cloud and the prominent landmark of the BT Tower.

Arriving at the bridleway, turn left for a few yards to a stone step stile over the wall and cross the fields to the Hanging Stone. Set on the very edge, this is a marvellous viewpoint. Gritstone steps descend to the base of the massive buttress, which has two memorial plaques, then you take the left fork down to the track. Turn right, then, beyond the farm, a path slants left to a stile and continues down across the field, past a large

Castle Rocks

boulder. Looking back there is a fine view of the Hanging Stone above the farm of the same name.

A stile leads into the larch wood and the path goes down the clough, through the trees, back to the river and Danebridge.

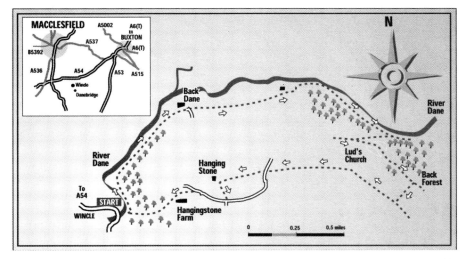

CULCHETH CLUB

Sign in Culcheth Linear Park

LOCATION: 3 miles north of Warrington
START: Culcheth Linear Park, off Wigshaw Lane, Culcheth
DISTANCE: 4½ miles
GRADE: Easy
TIME: 2 hours
BUS: 19 Warrington to Leigh
MAP: Pathfinder 723, Landranger 109
REFRESHMENTS: General Elliot

Culcheth comes from the Celtic 'narrow wood', and this is an appropriate name for the tree-lined park surrounding the former Wigan to Glazebrook railway. Trees are in short supply, though, in the surrounding countryside, for many hedges have vanished, leaving paths to zigzag along forgotten field boundaries. But the place thronged with a steady procession of walkers on our visit. Had there been a mass outbreak of hiking fever in Cheshire? Several "Hellos" later, we discovered it was the day of the sponsored walk for Croft County Primary School.

THE ROUTE

Starting from the Ranger Cabin, on the site of the old Culcheth Station, climb the steps to the right of the railway bridge and turn right along Wigshaw Lane, then go left down Glaziers Lane. Though the first bit is on the road, it gets better soon, for opposite Glaziers Lane Farm a stile by a gate leads into the fields.

The path follows the field edge, over a series of stiles, with a distant view of Risley Prison. Ignoring the first signpost, go right at the second, which points across the field, and continue along the edge of the next field. Isolated oaks, heavy with acorns, look down on the green expanse and ahead is the tower of Croft Church. Then, passing Brook House Farm, with its hay bales like giant shredded wheat, you turn left along Lady Lane.

Before reaching the sandstone church, which was built in the early 19th century, a footpath leads off to the right. After the first field, the route becomes indistinct, but continuing past a solitary willow by a pond, you come to a stile. Now the way follows an ancient lane, beneath arched hawthorns, until suddenly you emerge into a new housing estate.

Go right and right again, then fork left by the General Elliot pub, named after a general who fought in the Civil War. Opposite is all that remains of Croft Village School, which was built in 1872 and replaced an earlier Charity School. When the building was demolished, they found the dusty records of the first admissions register.

In a few yards, go left again, up Wildings Old Lane, then the right of way continues as a narrow grassy strip across the ploughed fields. After about a quarter of a mile, you make an abrupt right turn and the path continues past a couple of isolated hollow oak trees, the remnants of a former hedge, then zigzags on following the old field boundaries.

Reaching a tarmac road, go right and then left up the steps, and along the hedgerow. The path bends right, past a little pond, to join a grassy track, and this leads out to another road. Kenyon pumping station is concealed among the trees, and the route

Acorns

continues opposite, through a strip of oak, ash and sycamore. Then reaching the open fields, the path veers left. Joining a track you keep straight on and under the power lines, then steps lead down into Culcheth Linear Park.

The cast-iron signboards, made in Blackburn and featuring local history, are delightful, and turning right you follow the old Liverpool to Manchester railway. When it closed in 1968, this section of the route was part of Lancashire, but county reorganisation some six years later moved Culcheth and Croft into Cheshire. Reaching the bridge, there is then a choice of paths, high or low, back to the start.

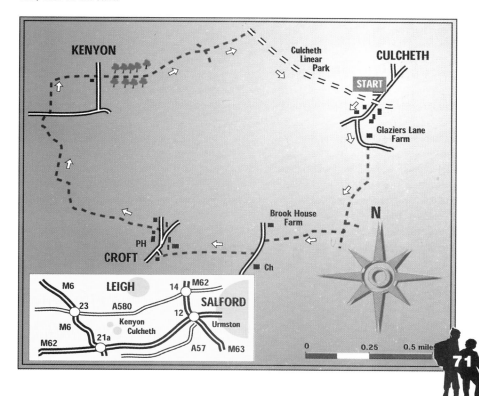

BRIDGE OF SIGHTS

Old Colliers Row

LOCATION: North Bolton

START: Barrow Bridge, off A58. Car park beyond bus-turning circle

DISTANCE: 4½ miles

GRADE: Moderate

TIME: 2½ hours

BUS: From Bolton 502 (not Sun)

MAP: Explorer - West Pennine Moors, Landranger 109

REFRESHMENTS: Pack a flask

Barrow Bridge is often described as a model village, but that doesn't mean it is very small and made of Lego. The cottages were purpose-built by an enlightened mill owner, and unlike those in the dark, back-to-backs of the towns, the workers here lived in a delightful country setting. Now the village is a conservation area and above the stream, that once powered the mills, rise the slopes of Smithills Country Park, while in the wooded cloughs the beech trees glow golden in the autumn sunshine.

THE ROUTE

From the car park, the site of a former mill reservoir, walk up the road beside the straightened Dean Brook and past the overlookers' cottages. Then at the bend, by Longshaw Ford Bridge, keep straight on beside the stream. Reaching the 63 Steps the climbing begins, and you follow the route of the 18th century quarrymen and miners, for whom this stone stairway was built.

Entering the 2000 acre Smithills Country Park, a broad, grassy path leads along the top of a little ridge to another kissing gate. Then the path continues across the field and beside the wall to Walker Fold, which dates back to the 17th century.

Cross straight over the road and follow the track above Walker Fold Woods. The trees were planted 40 years ago to prevent erosion, while grass has begun to cover the causey stones of this old mine road.

Reaching a gate at the end of the wood, you go left to join the higher path beneath Burnt Edge, so called because of its dark colour. A concrete pyramid covers an air shaft of the old colliery, and the path climbs on beside the wall. Ahead, the Winter Hill TV mast looks very close, but it is in fact well over a mile away.

Meeting a track, you turn right then, at the next signpost, head down to a stile into Holden Plantation. The path joins a track, and crossing the stream continues by the wall to Holdens Farm, where a fenced bridleway avoids the buildings.

With an autumnal nip in the air, even the horses had their winter coats on as we joined the lane. There are views over Bolton to the Peak District hills, then after passing the Sugar

Loaf, a grassed-over slag heap, the route goes right at a wooded clough.

The track leads down to Roscows Tenement Farm and, ignoring the signpost into the undergrowth, you go left between the buildings. The path continues across a clough, where once vines were grown and, after a stile by a gate, follows the fence to Sheep Cote Green Farm.

Continue along the farm road past Chadwick's Close Farm then, at the junction where a signpost helpfully indicates a right of way in every direction, you turn right. Passing the unoccupied Hampsons Farm, and the heather-covered disused Brownstones Quarry, which provided building sandstone, the main road is reached at Old Colliers Row. Turn left for a short way then, opposite the former school, go down Longshaw Ford Road.

This attractive lane descends by a strip of woodland, which offers softer walking than the tarmac: then, opposite the drive to Lower Tongs Farm, you turn left

Smithills Country Park

along an old lane. After passing Pendlebury's Farm, a signpost points down across the field towards the 252ft high Barrow Bridge Chimney. Aiming to the right of Sheep House Farm, you turn right on the track back to Barrow Bridge car park.

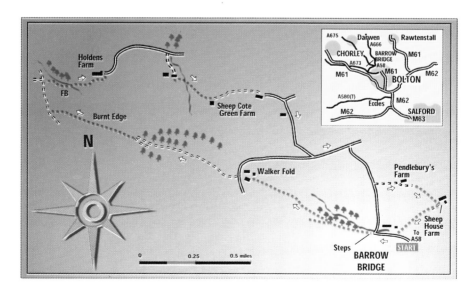

FORGING AHEAD

Park Bridge

LOCATION: 2 miles south of Oldham
START: Park Bridge, signed from A627.
Park by Visitor Centre, toilets
DISTANCE: 4 miles
GRADE: Easy
TIME: 2 hours
NOTE: Visitor Centre open weekends,
Tue, Wed & Thu afternoons
BUS: Oldham-Ashton 409
MAP: Pathfinder 713, Landranger 109
REFRESHMENTS: Daisy Bridge

"Any old iron?", goes the Victorian music hall song and there's plenty at Park Bridge, for this was the site of the iron works that produced rivets for the Eiffel Tower. But now the coal mines, the railway and the canal have all gone and the once industrial Medlock Valley is a peaceful wildlife refuge. Here beside the river you may glimpse the brilliant blue flash of a kingfisher, or spot a tree creeper in the woodland. With two Visitor Centres and a cafe to warm up in, this is a good walk for a chilly winter's day.

THE ROUTE

From Park Bridge Visitor Centre, which occupies the former stables of the Iron Works, walk down the tarmac road and over the River Medlock. Reaching Alt Hill Road, you turn uphill, past the Kennels and Cattery to the next junction, where a footpath climbs the steps. This leads to the disused railway and you turn right along the line that was built in 1861 to link Oldham, Ashton and Guide Bridge.

It is easy walking high above the valley with Hartshead Pike, which commemorates the marriage of Edward VII, prominent on the distant skyline. But the bridges are long gone, so you must switchback over the intervening road and footpaths that bisect the line.

After about half a mile, the railway crosses a high embankment above the attractively wooded Holden Clough. Turning right on the far side, you pass Limehurst Farm and continue down the track. To the east lie the Dark Peak moors and to the south is Manchester, while across the clough rises the turreted tower of Bardsley Church.

Reaching the busy Oldham Road, cross with care, then follow the track opposite. After 200 yards, a footpath leads over the fields and, crossing an old lane, continues on the fringe of Boodle Wood into Daisy Nook Country Park. The path then curves downhill through magnificent beech trees to join the disused Hollinwood Branch Canal, which was used to transport coal. (The Countryside Centre and cafe is only two minutes away to the left.)

Turn right along the Oldham Way, over the aqueduct, and up beside the remnants of former locks to Sammy's Basin, a large pool named after a water bailiff. Then reaching the Fairbottom Branch Canal, you go right. The water has almost vanished beneath the bulrushes - the Ashton Canals became unnavigable in 1948 and closed seven years later.

After crossing a bridge above Valley Farm, the path tunnels under the A627 to pass Kerfoot's Pharmaceutical Works. The bridleway and footpath now run parallel through the trees above the river to Fennyfield Bridge, the terminus of the canal. Turning right on the road for a few yards, you then follow the bridleway by the river. Emerging onto Waggon Road, the site of an old tramway, cross the footbridge then turn down the steps and up to a signpost, where you go right.

Sammy's Basin

Passing fenced enclosures around old coal mines, the path climbs across the heathery hillside, through larch and silver birch, with extensive views over the Medlock Valley. Reaching a steep sided little clough, you descend to a wooden bridge, and climb to cross the embankment of the old railway viaduct, which was demolished in 1971. Then it's downhill back to the site of Park Bridge Iron Works, which closed over 30 years ago and at its peak employed 800 people.

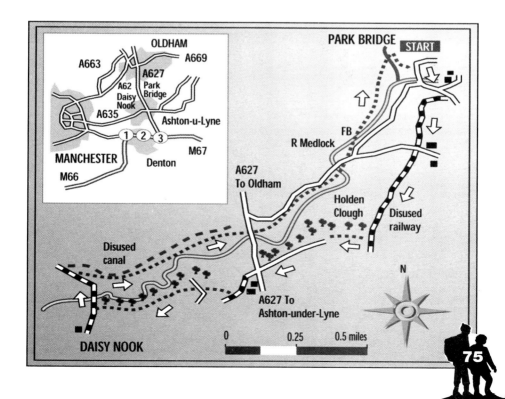

FIRE AND WATER

Cricketer's grave

LOCATION: South Cheshire

START: Nantwich, car park off A534, turn right just before the river

DISTANCE: 5 miles

GRADE: Easy

TIME: 2½ hours

TRAIN: Nantwich

MAP: Explorer 257, Landranger 118

REFRESHMENTS: Star Inn

When Nantwich caught fire, the flames raged for nearly three weeks, and when they went out there wasn't much left. Fortunately, the people were a bit more careful with tinderboxes after that and the classic black and white houses are now 400 years old. The inhabitants carried on living dangerously though, for this was the only Cheshire town to support Cromwell. But the battle fought here in 1644 was the turning point of the Civil War, and now the River Weaver meanders through a quiet countryside, while holiday barges ply the Shropshire Union Canal.

THE ROUTE

From the car park beside the River Weaver, walk back to the road bridge, which was built in 1803 by a local stonemason. Crossing the road you continue beside the river along Water Lode, where a plaque commemorates the Great Fire of Nantwich.

A more recent fire destroyed Nantwich Mill, and turning right over the old mill bridge, you follow the tarmac path to another bridge. The path continues upstream through Mill Fields, where the Domesday Book records a watermill, then crossing a third bridge you go under the Crewe to Shrewsbury railway line.

A strip of land leads between the river and Nantwich Lake until the A530 is met at Shrew Bridge. Turn right for a few yards, then go right again at the bridleway sign before Shrewbridge House. Crossing the field, you continue through a gate and keep straight on to another gate in the field corner. There is little sign of the Market Drayton branch line which closed in 1967, and following the fence brings you to the modern railway. Take care crossing, then follow the hedge to Green Lane and on over the canal bridge.

The tarmac leads out to Marsh Lane and turning left you follow the grassy verge for about a quarter of a mile. Reaching Dig Lane go right and, keeping straight on at the bend, the track leads between high hedges past Dorfold Dairy Farm. Continuing across open farmland, there are extensive views and, though the 17th century Dorfold Manor is hidden among the trees, there are some magnificent mature limes and sweet chestnuts on the estate.

Acton's 800-year-old church tower appears ahead and you keep straight on past a helpful way-mark pointing everywhere but down. Entering this tiny village, which in Saxon times was bigger than Nantwich, you pass the Star Inn and the old church with its unusual cricketer's grave. During the six week siege of Nantwich, the King's troops were garrisoned in Acton Church.

Turning right down Wilbraham Road, named after the first owner of Dorfold Hall, take the footpath on the left at the road bend. This leads across the fields to the Shropshire Union Canal, where you join the towpath and walk under the bridge. The wide canal was completed in 1779, but finishing at Nantwich proved financially disastrous and 56 years later it was extended to Birmingham.

1803 Bridge at Nantwich

Don't cross the bridge by the marina, the original canal terminus, but continue along the embankment to Telford's black and white cast iron aqueduct. Here you turn down the steps and follow the road back into Nantwich, past Malbank School and along Welsh Row. This was named after the Celts who came this way to sell their cattle and all tastes are catered for with half a dozen old pubs, several restaurants, a chip shop, bookshop and gallery.

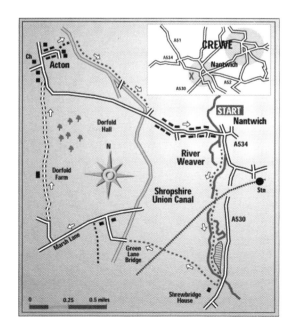

HIDDEN BEAUTIES

LOCATION: Bury
START: Clarence Park car park, off A56 Walmersley Road, at the end of Royal Avenue
DISTANCE: 4½ miles
GRADE: Moderate, but very muddy if wet
TIME: 2½ hours
BUS: From Bury 472
MAP: Pathfinder 701, Landranger 109
REFRESHMENTS: Clarence Park

Looking towards Knowl Hill

'The Forgotten Valley' is how Bury History Society's booklet describes the Cheesden Valley, and it is. Hidden away beyond the M66, the deep clough sees few visitors, yet once it powered 14 cotton mills and provided work for over 2000 people. Nearby Chesham was the home of several wealthy cotton masters who built their grand houses among the woods. But now the mansions are gone, and the stately beeches and Turkey oaks are home to thrushes, redwings, and scurrying flocks of tits and finches.

THE ROUTE

From the car park, walk up the steps to the Lido, with its gaggle of Canada geese, and go through the gateway on the right. A tarmac path then follows the iron railings to Clarence Wood where you turn right. Bearing left, a path leads through the trees and, after emerging briefly into a field, continues through Lower Lee Wood to Chesham Green Cottages.

Joining a track, turn left and follow it over the M66 and up past some houses to a T-junction. Go left and past Nineveh Farm then, at the bend, a stile leads right onto Walmersley Golf Course. Way-marks point up by the stream and, ignoring a misleading arrow, you cross the stile by Broomses Farm and walk up to the road.

The footpath opposite follows an old sunken lane across the fields until, at the second cross wall, you turn left. Gradually veering away from the wall, continue uphill, aiming for the prominent fencepost beside a wooden stepstile. This is a tremendous viewpoint, with Knowl Hill and Scout Moor to the north and Holcombe Tower to the west, while Bury and Manchester cover the plain to the south.

Keep straight on by the wall then, as the ground steepens, you slant down the heathery slope past a solitary sycamore to join Scotland Lane. Turn right and follow the old cobbled track high above Cheesden Brook. The name means the gravelly vale, and the solitary surviving chimney is from Washwheel Mill, originally a calico printers, then a paper mill and finally a bleachworks closing in 1919.

A tall radio mast appears ahead, but stay along the rim of the gorge heading towards Rochdale and the distant Pennine Moors. Then, reaching a patch of tarmac, you go right down an old lane. Keep straight on, past the Normandie Hotel and Old Birtle, along the bridleway.

Approaching Harwood Fields Farm, the mud gets deeper, then the farm drive is followed out to the road. The footpath opposite descends to a stile, and continues beside the fence. This valley can be very wet, so squelch your way down to below Hercules Farm to a squeezer stile by a gate. Forking left, a path then descends through the wooded clough until, reaching Gorsey House, the farm track leads down and under the motorway.

Turn right up the tarmac track, then go left between the hawthorn hedges. Reaching the bend, you turn right to re-enter Chesham Woods with its pollarded Manchester poplars, once planted as a windbreak.

Keep to the right of the stream, then go over a bridge. Crossing a broad track, you continue through stone gateposts into Chesham House Wood, whose magnificent beech trees are a

Horses on Scotland Lane

century old, though the house was demolished in 1959. Keep left to a stile, then follow the fence past a new plantation to a footbridge into Clarence Wood, and back to the Lido.

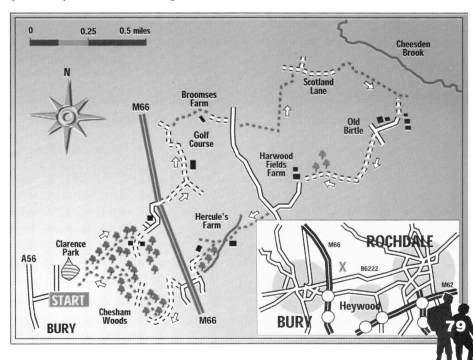

REDES ALL ABOUT IT

Capesthorne Hall

LOCATION: 7 miles south of Wilmslow

START: Redes Mere. Lay-by on minor road off A34, beyond Capesthorne Hall, signed Henbury

DISTANCE: 3 miles

GRADE: Easy, but can be muddy

TIME: 1½ hours

NOTE: Capesthorne Hall, open March to October

MAP: Pathfinder 759, Landranger 118

REFRESHMENTS: Pack a flask

Pheasants clattered off into the undergrowth, and shy coots gave their sharp calls as we scuffed through the saw-toothed leaves of the sweet chestnuts beside Redes Mere. This is Bromley-Davenport country, the Cheshire family which for centuries kept law and order in Macclesfield Forest, safeguarding the game and hunting rights. But the Redes Mere ducks are not the shy, retiring sort. They have trained passing motorists to arrive with a constant supply of bread, and if you haven't brought any, they will be very disappointed.

THE ROUTE

Braving the ducks and swans, walk along the lane beside the lake, which is aptly named for Redes Mere means the reedy pool. Then, reaching the sign to Capesthorne, you turn left across the field. The path follows the edge of the wood, where siskin, nuthatch, tree creepers and tits can be seen.

Keeping straight on at the path junction, continue through the trees, and past the Sailing Club. Follow the track to the end of the lake where a footpath sign points left, over the dam. Though Redes Mere started life as a natural pool, it was extended to form a reservoir for the Capesthorne Park lakes.

Crossing the busy A34, take the path opposite, and this leads along the edge of a field where lapwings, plovers and flocks of over-wintering finches feed. The path continues beside the first of the Capesthorne lakes, which are fished for tench, roach, carp, pike and bream. On the far side of the water is a brick pillar topped with a stone sphere, marking the site of the 15th century hall, demolished in 1722 when the present mansion was built.

Continuing by the second lake, there is an impressive vista of Capesthorne Hall, whose ornate front was rebuilt in 1861 after a terrible fire. Passing the five-arched ornamental bridge, constructed some 20 years earlier, you go by the old saw mill, then joining a track this leads out to Mill Lane.

Follow the way-marked path opposite, trending left to a stile, and over the next field, which we found strewn with giant puffballs. Then, crossing a grassy track, at a stile by a gate, you squeeze over a stile just beyond and turn sharp left beside the hedge. Follow this round to a way-marked telegraph pole, where you turn right.

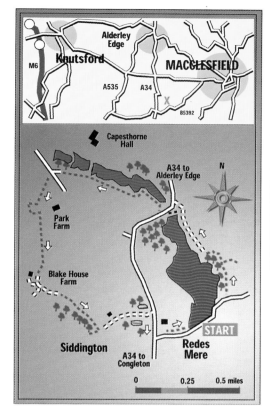

Boathouse, Capesthorne Lake

Keep a sharp eye on the way-marks, for these will guide you over stiles to a muddy track. Quitting this (thankfully!) in a few yards, you then aim to the left of Blake House Farm to join the farm drive. Follow this past the buildings, then turn left along the unsurfaced track.

Passing the house, the bridleway leads above the wooded valley of Snape Brook until, reaching a T-junction, you go left. Continue past a thatched Hansel and Gretel cottage, which sells hand-made toys, then joining a track, this leads past some gloomy pools, and out to the main road.

Turn right along the pavement, past Siddington Village Hall, which was once the village school, then go left down Fanshawe Lane. The road can soon be avoided by going left into the picnic area where, with a distant view of the Peak District hills, a path leads back to the mere. An information board will help you identify the water birds, but it doesn't mention the large white ducks with orange bills, which are geese-mallard hybrids.

GRAVE CONCERN

Misty church in Hepstonstall

LOCATION: 3 miles north west of Hebden Bridge
START: Hardcastle Crags NT car park on the Widdop road, 2 miles beyond Heptonstall
DISTANCE: 5 miles
GRADE: Moderate
TIME: 3 hours
MAP: Outdoor Leisure - South Pennines, Landranger 103
REFRESHMENTS: Heptonstall

Above Hebden Bridge, only shadowy shapes could be seen in the mist. Briefly the sun peeped through, and a cockerel crowed its delight, then the grey murk closed around us once more. At Eaves Rocks, a helpful couple described what we should have seen, and in Heptonstall the swirling fog in the churchyard had all the atmosphere of a Hitchcock film. But it was a splendid walk, with an excellent excuse to come again. Perhaps next time we'll see the view!

THE ROUTE

From the car park, take the track opposite that leads uphill, then just before Clough House a way-mark points left across the field. A signpost is reached and you join an old hollow way, which is followed up through two narrow gates and past the ruined Clough Head farm. Another way-mark points on, slanting left to the head of the clough where, crossing a stile and a bridge, you climb to join the Pennine Way.

Gradually veering away from the wall, we followed the grassy track across the bleak heather moor, while a startled grouse gave his "Go back!" cry of alarm. Reaching Mount Pleasant, the Pennine Way turns right beside the wall then, passing Long High Top, you go through a little wooden gate and the descent begins. Channelled between stone walls, the path leads down, across a tarmac lane and on down, over another road, to a farmhouse at Colden.

Here the Pennine Way goes briefly left, but watch for the downhill continuation in the far corner of the field where a grassy track descends to the deep Colden Valley. Just before reaching Colden Water, with its ancient clapper bridge, you turn left along the Calderdale Way. This follows an old causey path through Foster Wood to a stone step stile, and continues over the fields. Reaching a gateway, the path kinks and continues beside the wall to join a green lane, where you turn uphill.

At the T-junction, go right and behind the house, then keep straight on at the next junction along a walled track. Stay on the upper track at the fork, then joining a tarmac lane you follow this uphill. Just before the bend, the Calderdale Way continues into Eaves Wood. Threading between huge boulders and gnarled oaks, the path keeps to the top edge of the wood until, reaching Eaves Rocks from which there are spectacular views over Mytholm and the River Calder, you turn left into Heptonstall.

Keep straight on past the Victorian church, then climb the steps on the left to the ruins of the former 13th century church. Continuing by the Old Grammar School Museum, you turn left, past the Old Cloth Hall, where local cloth was sold, then opposite Weavers Square, you go right along Townfield Lane.

Follow the track over the fields and through a gate, then at the next gateway veer left to a squeezer stile and out to the road. Turn left, then in a few

Hebden Dale

yards take the footpath signed Hardcastle Crags. The path stays high above the steep-sided Hebden Dale until, meeting a track, you cross the wall and continue along the field edge. The path soon leads back into the trees and you walk through a stand of mature beeches to enter the NT land. Continue across the steep slope to join a good track above the 200-year-old Gibson Mill, then it is an easy climb back up to the car park.

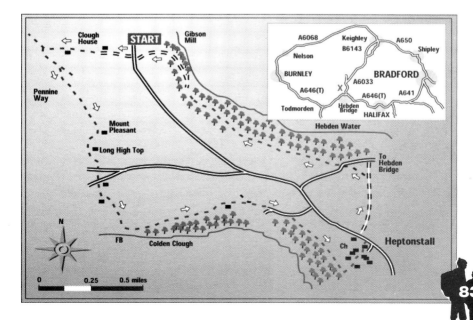

FOLLOW THE TRUTH PATH

Mellor Church

LOCATION: Marple, near Stockport
START: The grassy triangle between B6101 & B6102, roadside parking
DISTANCE: 6 miles
GRADE: Moderate
TIME: 3 hours
BUS: 358 from Stockport
TRAIN: Marple
MAP: Outdoor Leisure - Dark Peak, Landranger 109
REFRESHMENTS: Roman Lakes

High above Marple, and with a view stretching to Lyme Park, Mellor Church makes an excellent objective for a walk. The name comes from the Celtic for smooth-topped hill, and the first church was built on the grassy summit by the invading Saxons. Once an industrial area, the textile mills are long gone and only the old mill lodges remain, grandly renamed the Roman Lakes. But the highlight of the walk is the little pack-horse bridge that spans the Goyt, built by Samuel Oldknow for his mill workers 200 years ago.

THE ROUTE

The sign to the Roman Lakes points along Faywood Drive, and continuing down the track brings you to Bottoms Bridge. Turn right and follow Lake Road where, in 1793, Oldknow built his six-storied cotton mill. This was destroyed by fire 100 years later, but going right again you pass Bottom's Hall, built as a farm and dormitory for the apprentices.

The track continues past the Roman Lakes, where there is a cafe and toilets. This former mill pond was constructed on the original line of the River Goyt. Follow the track under the railway arches then, 100 yards past the octagonal house, you turn sharp left along the Cown Edge Way. The path climbs, then crossing the railway bridge, continues over Mellor and Townscliffe Golf Course. Helpful way-marks point the route beside a wooded clough until, reaching a signpost, you turn left.

Crossing a track, the path continues past Linnet Clough Scout Camp over a field and down into a wooded clough. Emerging into the open, you pass some inquisitive goats, then reaching Damsteads Farm, the track leads out to the road.

A narrow path opposite descends to cross a deep clough, then climbs to join a lane. Turning right, this leads to Knowle Farm where you go through a little gate and follow the fence up to Mellor Church. The 15th century tower is the earliest part of the building, with foundations dating back to Norman times, while the oak pulpit, carved from a single tree, is probably the oldest in Britain.

From the churchyard, another path heads straight down the hillside, then crossing the clough at a footbridge, you climb out to the road. Almost opposite, a footpath leads past a small mill pond and continues across the fields. Keep straight on up Whetmorehurst Lane, then at the bend take the path that contours across the hillside and past the golf course.

Reaching a track, you turn right to descend by the wall, then bearing right follow the winding pack-horse lane

Roman Bridge

downhill. Crossing a track, keep straight on down to a T-junction where you turn right, then after the house go left to continue the descent into the valley.

At the railway embankment, a sharp right turn leads past Windy Bottom Farm, and through a long tunnel. The track continues by the swiftly flowing River Goyt, then you go left over the picturesque 'Roman' Bridge.

Don't climb the steps, but continue upstream to the houses and follow the track up to the main road. Crossing over, you continue up Plucksbridge Road where steps lead to the Peak Forest Canal, which was commissioned by Oldknow and opened in 1797. Turning right, the towpath is followed for about a mile, then reaching Brick Bridge, you cross over and walk past Marple Moorings. On the far side of the canal junction bridge, a flight of locks leads down to the main road where you turn right, back to the grassy triangle.

HEAD FOR THE HILLS

LOCATION: West side of Blackburn

START: Witton Country Park car park, off A674, toilets

DISTANCE: 6 miles

GRADE: Moderate, one very muddy spot

TIME: 3 hours

NOTE: Visitor Centre open Thu-Sun, daily in summer

BUS: From Blackburn 11, 123, 124 & 152

TRAIN: Millhill

MAP: Explorer-West Pennine Moors, Landranger 103

REFRESHMENTS: Butlers Arms & Visitor Centre tearoom

Viewpoint on the Yellow Hills

Enfolded by a great loop of the River Darwen, the woods and meadows of Witton Country Park are a delight. Here on the fringe of Blackburn over a hundred different species of birds have been seen, while the Visitor Centre has a surprise in store with its wildlife zoo. There are field voles and bank voles, wood mice and house mice and even a ship's rat. But our favourites were the tiny harvest mice. Beautifully displayed amongst ears of corn, each weighs less than a 2p coin.

THE ROUTE

From the car park follow the tarmac drive past the sports pavilion until, just before the Visitor Centre, you turn right through the red rose gates. A yew avenue leads past the lily pond of Witton House (demolished in 1954), then, reaching a small car park, you turn left into Big Cover Wood.

Keeping left, follow the good path up through the trees, then emerging into the open, continue over the fields to Under Billinge Lane. A few yards to the left, a path enters Billinge Wood and climbs gently until, reaching a car park, you turn left out into the field.

Aim for the knoll ahead (actually the top of a small quarry and a marvellous viewpoint). To the north lies the Forest of Bowland, westwards is Morecambe Bay, while to the south are Winter Hill and Darwen Tower.

Continuing along the ridge, known as the Yellow Hills after the gorse that blooms here, you follow the fence down beside Butler's Delph Quarry to a track. Go left for a few yards, then right on a footpath into the trees, but in 50 yards watch for an indistinct fork right, which leads out to a stile.

Heading straight across the fields through a couple of gates, the path joins a track, then reaching the lane, you take the footpath opposite and follow the hedge to a stile on the right of the new house. Turn left, then going through a gap, keep to the left of the hedge and continue in the same direction to a stile by a wooded ravine. The next bit can be very muddy, but descending into the morass you can at least assured there is nothing worse beyond!

The path veers right to join a track above the tree-lined River Darwen, one of the major tributaries of the River Ribble. The difficulties are now over, and after descending to the river, a track leads to a stile by Lower Park Farm.

Follow the farm drive to the footbridge, but instead of crossing, turn left along a good track beside the river. On the skyline to the right are the roofs of Hoghton Tower, a 16th century fortified mansion. As the track bends away, the footpath continues along the bank to a single span bridge where you go left then, in 100 yards, a stile leads onto the 18-hole golf course. After following the wall, the path continues beside the fence across the fields and over Throstle Nest Brow into Pleasington.

Crossing the road between the Butlers Arms and the magnificent Roman Catholic Priory, opened in 1819, you follow the fenced path on across the fields and over the playing field to Butler's Bridge. Don't cross, but follow the river upstream back to the car park, or detour left to see the woodman and the zoo at the Visitor Centre.

Head of the Woodman

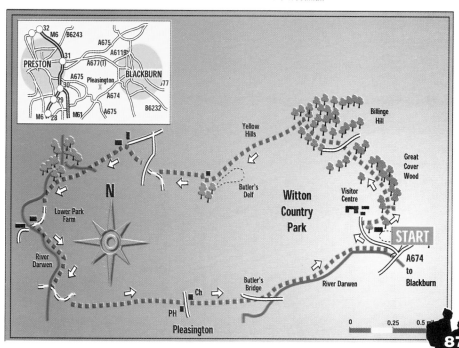

LEGENDS OF ROCK

Raven Rock

LOCATION: Between Buxton and Leek

START: Roadside parking, off A53 on minor road from Upper Hulme (Grid reference 004621)

DISTANCE: 4 miles

GRADE: Moderate

TIME: Two hours

MAP: Outdoor Leisure - White Peak, Landranger 118 & 119

REFRESHMENTS: Paddock Farm (closed Mon & Tue in winter)

On the border of the Staffordshire Moorlands, forming the skyline above the town of Leek, rises the striking profile of Hen Cloud and the Roaches. There is the look of the high hills about these summits and, standing on the edge, with the valley of the River Dane spread out below, the view is indeed worthy of a mountain. A landscape of heather, bilberry and weather-sculpted gritstone rocks stretches away into the distance, a red grouse skims low over the moor with its gruff complaining call, and above is the constantly changing sky.

THE ROUTE

From the layby, a track leads gently uphill to Rock Hall. This gamekeeper's cottage, built into the cliff, was converted to a climbing hut in memory of Don Whillans, who pioneered many hard climbs at the Roaches. Turning left in front of the cottage, follow the path through the fringe of pine trees and beneath the towering mass of Raven Rock to a flight of gritstone steps.

These make easy work of the ascent, until reaching the top you come to a seat. Carved from a solid block of stone and with just enough room for two, it is poised on the very edge of the cliff, so take care. Close by, a plaque commemorates the visit of the Princess of Teck, the mother of Queen Mary.

You are now on the Terrace and above is the Great Slab, a smooth wall of rock topped by a huge overhang. Here is the most spectacular, and one of the most intimidating, climbs at the Roaches. Don Whillan's classic goes directly over the rock ceiling, and as the climber hangs upside down from fingers and toes, it is easy to see why it is known as The Sloth.

Reaching the end of the Terrace, the path climbs between the rocks to the top of the escarpment. All is now easy, a stroll gently gaining height until Doxey Pool is reached. The pool was named after the daughter of Bess Bowyer, who lived at Rock Hall. One night, it is said, strange men came and carried her off and Bess died from grief. There have been many strange men since, and not just the climbers, for until recently the self-styled Lord of the Roaches lived a reclusive existence at Rock Hall.

From the pool to the summit is about a mile, and standing beside the trig point at 1658ft you look east to the Staffordshire moors, while to the west is the distant escarpment of Bosley Cloud and the sentinel finger of the communications tower atop Croker Hill.

Now it is gently downhill as the path weaves a way through gritstone rocks carved into mysterious shapes by thousands of years of wind and weather, and the

Climber on Right Route

road is reached at Roach End.

Turning right, it is about a mile and a half along the quiet, unfenced lane, then after the cattle-grid you take the footpath which passes Shawtop. A track is joined and you turn right. When this bends left to the farm, a narrow path continues through the heather until, passing between the Roaches and Hen Cloud, the track is re-joined by Rock Hall to complete a walk through some of the finest scenery in Staffordshire.

Roach End

Whaley Bridge
MACCLESFIELD
A5002   BUXTON
A54   A515
Upper   A53
Hulme
A523   X
A520   LEEK

The Roaches

N

Shawtop

Doxey Pool

Rockhall

START

To A53 via Upper Hulme

89

RESERVOIR TRODS

LOCATION: Newhey, 4 miles east of Rochdale

START: Ogden Lane, off A640. NWW car park on Private Road by the dam, toilets

DISTANCE: 4 miles

GRADE: Moderate

TIME: 2 hours

BUS: From Rochdale 451 (not Sun)

TRAIN: Newhey station, one mile

MAP: Outdoor Leisure - South Pennines, Landranger 109

REFRESHMENTS: Tea room open Sunday afternoons

Looking across the Piethorne Reservoir

With the reservoirs in the Piethorne Valley, near Rochdale, reflecting a clear, blue sky, it was a perfect winter's day. Yet there was no-one about, and even the little Pennine village of Lower Ogden seemed deserted. Then we spotted Simon. "Come in and I'll put the kettle on," he said, "would you like some fruit cake?" Forty years ago, his parents restored the magnificent old farmhouse, turning the outbuildings into a craft centre and tea room. With a welcome like that, how could we refuse?

THE ROUTE

Follow the tarmac track from the entrance to the car park up onto the dam of Ogden Reservoir. This was constructed in the 1870s to supply Oldham with drinking water, and from high above Foulwater Lodge you look down on Newhey. On the far side, steps climb to join a track and turning right, this leads beside Rough Bank Plantation, which conceals disued 19th century coal mines.

From the corner of the wood, a path goes right, to cross the stream, and you climb past the ruins of Rag Hole Farm to meet a grassy track. Turning right, Kitcliffe Reservoir soon comes into view, then, in about 400 yards, watch for a yellow arrow pointing left.

Heading uphill, soon an obvious track appears and this is followed across the hillside, past a solitary sycamore and the ruins of Binns. Only a few stones now mark the large farming community which dated back to the 13th century but was abandoned when the reservoirs came.

Keep along the hillside, above Piethorne Reservoir, until the track fizzles out and you enter Old House Ground Plantation. This mixed woodland, planted about 90 years ago, is now a Nature Reserve belonging to the Lancashire Wildlife Trust. The path leads along the top edge, until reaching a kissing gate, you turn downhill, past the cataracts from Norman Hill Reservoir which lies above.

The track goes past the old Limehouse, once used to store lime for adding to the feeder stream to reduce the acidity of the water, then, crossing the end of the trout-stocked Piethorne Reservoir, continues up the hill to a T-junction.

Turn right and carry on over the dam of Hanging Lees Reservoir until, at the corner, you cross an ancient metal ladder stile and head straight up the grassy hillside. Yellow arrows mark the route and soon a track materialises which leads above the 79ft deep Rooden Reservoir, built a century ago.

Looking back, Windy Hill mast is prominent on the skyline while to the south-east, beyond Denshaw Church, the outline of the Pots and Pans Memorial can be seen against the Saddleworth Moors. Ahead are the masts on Crow Knowl, and the track leads past a new house at Edge Gate,

Through the gatepost

rebuilt after a fire. Continuing past Ogden Edge Farm, dated 1771, you fork right at the next junction.

With a view over Rochdale to Knowl Hill and the distant moors, the track then leads gently downhill to Higher Ogden. Bending left, past the early 18th century School House, the tarmac continues down to Lower Ogden whose stone mullioned farmhouse, barn and stables date from around 1710.

Then, when you can drag yourself away from the tea room and Shippon Craft Centre, a footpath opposite leads down to the car park at Springmill, whose toilet block was once the Weighbridge offices for the local coalmine.

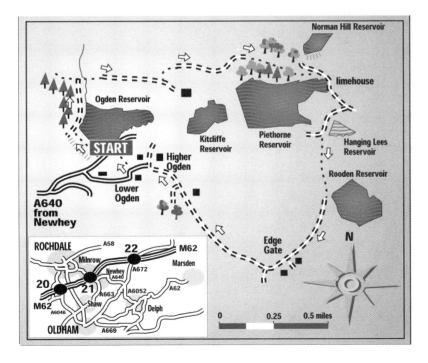

WALK 43: SANDBACH FLASHES (4 MILES, EASY)
FLASHES OF INSPIRATION

Relaxing at the Bears Paw

LOCATION: South Cheshire

START: The Bears Paw, Warmingham, 3 miles south of Middlewich. Park behind pub

DISTANCE: 4 (or 3) miles

GRADE: Easy

TIME: 2 hours

MAP: Pathfinder 775, Landranger 118

REFRESHMENTS: Bears Paw

Watching a pair of great crested grebes as they rose breast to breast from the water in their magnificent courtship dance was the highlight of our walk around Sandbach Flashes. These shallow lakes, formed by salt pumping subsidence, are a haven for many species of wildfowl. There are coots, swans, mallards and moorhens all breeding here, while bullfinches, chaffinches and assorted tits feed among the surrounding willows and alders. This is a walk among the wildlife, and such a display is not to be missed, so don't forget your binoculars.

THE ROUTE

Leaving the Bears Paw, turn left to follow School Lane over the River Wheelock, and past the old corn mill with its Craft Workshops. At first there is no pavement, but one materialises by the entrance to Warmingham Grange. Just before the primary school, turn right over an awkward stile into the fields.

Passing a white dovecote, continue by the hedge until, at the next gate, you go left to an ancient ladder stile. Joining the road, turn right to the wide-verged Green Lane, which leads past Ryecroft Cottage and a notice warning of subsidence. The lane then dips by Moston Flash, the first of the salt flashes which are all protected as SSSIs (Sites of Special Scientific Interest). These water-filled depressions, now very popular with anglers, were created when the ground sank due to pumping from natural brine springs for salt extraction.

Before you reach the 'Road Clear' sign, turn right over a stile and bear left to the next stile. Aiming diagonally across the field, next follow the hedge out to the road. Turn right, then immediately after Yew Tree Farm, go left beside a marshy wood. On this old path, known locally as Warblers Walk, we met a birdwatcher who told us of long-tailed tits and a great spotted woodpecker among the trees.

Emerging onto the road, turn right to pass The Moat. Here we looked in vain for the kingfisher and the water rail, but above our heads the siskins were feeding in the alder carr.

92

Continuing over the next road, you arrive at the 93 mile long Trent and Mersey Canal. Turn right along the waterway, which links the River Trent to Preston Brook and was opened in 1777, then in 200 yards, watch for the footpath which shortcuts across the field to the road bend.

Birdwatching, Watch Lane Flash

The longer walk, however, follows the canal to the next bridge where you go right for a few yards by the Phosphorus works, then right again to follow Red Lane. Passing Watch Lane Flash, this is a good bird watching site, for the extensive reed beds create an ideal nesting habitat for water birds.

Follow the tarmac road round the bend, and keep straight on down Watch Lane. Then, going through another car park, the unsurfaced track continues past Isle Pool, and the red brick Watchlane Farm. Turning right at the T-junction, you pass Limerick Hill Cottage, and there is a good view of Crabmill Flash. Then a footpath sign points left, over a farmer's obstacle course of heaped up hard core, and you turn right along the field edge.

Even after heavy downpours the fields are not too muddy and soon you are back in Warmingham. The name means Wyrma's place, but before being embraced by the Bears Paw have a look at the church. When it was rebuilt, they kept their 17th century church tower, hence the rhyme: "Poor Warmingham, proud people, new church and old steeple".

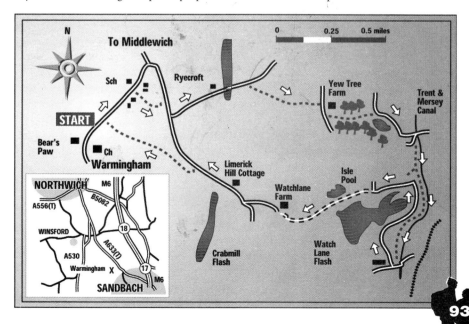

WHY? OH! WAYOH?

Beside Wayoh Resevoir

LOCATION: 5 miles north of Bolton

START: NWW car park off B6391 above Entwistle Reservoir, at end of tarmac track

DISTANCE: 4½ miles

GRADE: Moderate, with some moorland walking

TIME: 2½ hours

BUS: Bolton to Chapeltown: 563 (not Sun)

TRAIN: Entwistle

MAP: Explorer - West Pennine Moors, Landranger 109

REFRESHMENTS: Chetham Arms

Prehistoric man always had an eye for the high places and the site he chose for a stone circle, up on the moors above Bolton's chain of reservoirs, still has a wild and windswept atmosphere. Then, descending to the picturesque village of Chapeltown, you emerge by the Chetham Arms, named after the local 17th century benefactor who founded a school and library in Manchester. And the walk concludes with an easy stroll beside Wayoh Reservoir and through the lovely Armsgrove Clough.

THE ROUTE

Crossing the stepstile to the right of the car park entrance, follow the footpath up across the field. A way-marked post indicates a right fork, and Turton and Entwistle Reservoir comes into view. Originally built in 1838, to ensure a constant flow of water to the bleach works, the reservoir now supplies thirsty Bolton.

The path contours along the hillside, following a ruined wall above Tarkingtons Plantation until you meet a new track, which leads up to Greens Arms Road. Turn right, for about 100 yards, then take the footpath left into the wood.

After bending left, the track emerges from the pine trees and slants up the hill to the top of the next plantation. Already you are high above the valley, with expansive views to the long ridge of Holcombe Moor and the Peel Tower.

A track, the ancient Heights Lane, leads to a stile in the wall, and you continue beside a ruined wall across the hillside. Reaching a path junction, turn uphill to climb gently over the moor towards the masts atop the distant Winter Hill.

There is no mistaking the next objective, for a solid cast iron post marks the waterboard's empire, and here you turn left along the top of Cheetham Close. A path traverses the sea of winter-bleached grassland to a stile, and beyond only a few stones now mark the site of the stone circle, which was destroyed by 19th century vandals. But from the whitewashed trig point there is a view of Bolton spread out below.

The clear path continues along the hilltop to meet a wall, where you turn left and head

Windswept tree on Heights Lane

downhill to a beech wood. Passing to the right of a large barn, Jumbles Reservoir can be seen in the valley below. Then, crossing a track, you continue down beside an attractive clough to an old mill.

After crossing the Blackburn to Bolton Line into the old station yard, a cobbled lane leads downhill. In 100 yards, you fork left and emerge into the fleshpots of Chapeltown by the Chetham Arms, with its coat of arms dated 1746.

Turn left past Chetham Farm Cottage, which has mullioned windows, and the old school house, which also has a coat of arms. A few yards after the pavement ends, Embankment Road leads down to Wayoh Reservoir. This was built in 1876, and enlarged in 1962 when the Treatment Works was added. Turning left, a good path follows the water's edge, past Nature Conservation Areas, where wildfowl hide from visitors. Don't cross the causeway, but continue on the way-marked footpath up Armsgrove Clough under the nine-arched Railway Viaduct.

The path then forks right to Entwistle car park and, reaching the dam, you turn left to the road bend where a flight of steps leads back to the upper car park.

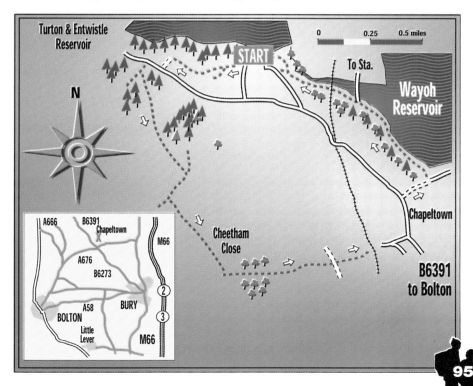

SUMMIT CHURNING

Frozen waterspout Cracken Edge Quarry

LOCATION: 5 miles east of Disley
START: Chinley Station, off B6062. Park on Station Road
DISTANCE: 4½ miles
GRADE: Moderate, but with an initial steep ascent.
TIME: 3 hours
TRAIN: Chinley
MAP: Outdoor Leisure - Dark Peak, Landranger 110
REFRESHMENTS: Chinley

Chinley was once a Mecca for ramblers, and weekends in the 1940s were so busy that a 10-minute religious service was held on the railway platform every Sunday. It's a bit quieter these days, but the long ridge of Chinley Churn still has a magnetic appeal, rising above the town like a huge crested wave. Old gritstone quarries spill piles of tumbled stone down the hillside, while a deserted farm looks out towards Kinder. But be sure to choose a clear day for your walk, as the views are magnificent.

THE ROUTE

Leaving Chinley Station, turn left to follow Station Road to the Squirrels Hotel, then go left again and over the railway. Turning right at the T-junction, you follow Maynestone Road for about 200 yards, then a narrow walled path leads left between the houses. It is a steep ascent, straight up the hillside and soon you are looking down on the roofs of Chinley, which means the clearing in a deep valley.

At last the angle eases and, joining an old lane, you turn right. Then, in a few yards, a track goes left to Cracken Edge Farm. Leaving the farm track at the bend, keep straight on and climb past a cottage to a stile, and continue to a small gate. There is now little sign of the right of way, but veering right, you climb the grass-covered quarry spoil to join a higher path, which runs along a shelf beneath the steep slopes of Chinley Churn.

The white scut of a startled rabbit vanished among the rocks as we continued along the edge, while across the wide bowl of the valley lay Mount Famine and the steep scarp slope of South Head. Cracken Edge Quarry was working until the late 1920s, and the path leads past numerous little quarries, before climbing again above the winding gear of an old incline.

It is now an airy promenade past huge piled-up blocks and neat retaining walls beside the top tier of the quarries. This is where the better stone was extracted by underground mining to make paving slabs and roofing slates.

After a stile by a gate, the path begins to descend, past the deserted cottage of Whiterakes. Ahead is the vast expanse of Kinder with the point of Edale Rocks prominent on the skyline beside the hunched shape of Swine's Back.

Joining a good track, you

Winding gear, Craken Edge Quarry

turn uphill again, and passing Higher Hills Cottage the track continues over the moor. Cresting the top of the ridge, there is a fine view over Little Hayfield to Lantern Pike and Coombes Edge, then reaching a signposted bridleway junction, you turn left.

The old walled lane crosses the bleak, grassy moor, with an extensive panorama over New Mills to Lyme Park, whose Cage appears on the skyline. Then keeping straight on at the next junction, past several depressions which were trial holes for coal, Whaley Bridge and the distant gleam of Toddbrook Reservoir come into view.

Joining Over Hill Road by Throstle Bank Farm, you descend steeply past Dryclough Farm, and turn right at Stubbins Lea House. A footpath then leads down across a little park to a bridge over the railway, which was once advertised as the most beautiful in Britain. It is then only a short way left, along the B6062, back to Station Road.

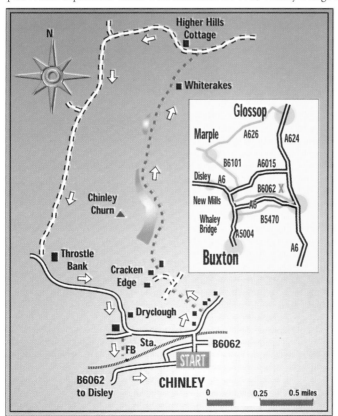

Notes

Public Transport Details

Many of the walks in this guide can easily be reached using buses, trains and Metrolink. When you leave the car at home, the day out starts the minute you leave the house, and you'll be surprised how much more you see when somebody else does the driving. Try the following special tickets...

Rail Ranger: As many train journeys as you wish in Greater Manchester, after 9.30am weekdays and all day weekends and Bank Holidays. £2.45

Evening Ranger: as above, for evenings. £1.25

Day Saver (Bus): Lets you travel on almost any bus in Greater Manchester, no matter which company runs it. Start as early as you like, available from the driver on your first trip. £3

Wayfarer: Allows a day's travel after 9.30am on weekdays and all day weekends and Bank Holidays. Available for almost every bus, train and Metrolink throughout Greater Manchester, parts of Lancashire, Cheshire, Staffordshire and the Peak District. The Wayfarer ticket also allows a discount at many attractions. Must be bought in advance from GMPTE Travelshops, staffed stations and Post Offices. £6.60 (adult), £3.30 (children and OAPs)

For more details, visit a GMPTE Travelshop at bus stations in Greater Manchester, ring the Public Transport Enquiry Bureau on 0161-228 7811 (8am-7pm, every day) or visit the internet journey planner on **www.gmpte.gov.uk**

Prices shown are correct at August 1999.